P9-BYK-311

Produced by Carlton Books
20 Mortimer Street
London, W1N 7RD

First published in hardback edition in 2001 by Chelsea House Publishers, a subsidiary of Haights Cross Communications. Printed and bound in Dubai.

3 5 7 8 6 4 2

The Chelsea House World Wide Web address is http://www.chelseahouse.com

Library of Congress Cataloging-in-Publication Data applied for

The Early Years –1949	ISBN: 0-7910-6084-5
The 50s	ISBN: 0-7910-6085-3
The 60s	ISBN: 0-7910-6086-1
The 70s	ISBN: 0-7910-6087-X
The 80s	ISBN: 0-7910-6088-8
The 90s	ISBN: 0-7910-6089-6

20TH CENTURY Pop Culture

THE 70s

Dan Epstein

Chelsea House Publishers
Philadelphia

20TH CENTURY
Pop Culture

The Early Years to 1949

The 50s

The 60s

The 80s

The 90s

Contents

nineteen 70

With the **killings at Kent State on May 4**, the divisions between the political left and right, between the **anti- and pro-war factions**, between the young and the old all seemed to grow ever wider. In the spring of 1970, anti-war demonstrations were part of virtually every college commencement ceremony in the country. Vassar grads wore **peace signs** on their gowns and mortarboards, while Tufts students boycotted their official ceremony to stage their own program.

TOP TELEVISION SHOWS

- *Marcus Welby, MD*
- *Gunsmoke*
- *Here's Lucy*
- *Bonanza*
- *Laugh-In*

'70 The Carpenters.

'70 The President meets The King.

The Tufts ceremony featured Simon and Garfunkel songs and a tribute to Tufts alumni killed in Southeast Asia. Even small-town schools got into the act; at Wilson college in Chambersburg, Pennsylvania, students greeted guest of honor Mamie Eisenhower with placards depicting black-shrouded skulls.

Troubled Water

Not surprisingly, the tension in the air made its way into the music. In July, Crosby, Stills, Nash, and Young followed their version of Joni Mitchell's hopeful "Woodstock" with the release of Neil Young's scathing "Ohio;" the song, which placed blame for the deaths of the four Kent State students directly on the doorstep of the White House, made it to number fourteen in the pop charts. The Temptations scored a number three pop hit the same month with "Ball of Confusion (That's What The World Is Today)," a single that seemed like a polite understatement next to Edwin Starr's angry "War," which spent three weeks at the top of the charts in September.

TOP SINGLES

Simon and Garfunkel
"Bridge Over Troubled Water"

The Jackson Five
"I'll Be There"

BJ Thomas
"Raindrops Keep Fallin' On My Head"

George Harrison
"My Sweet Lord"

The Carpenters
"(They Long To Be) Close To You"

Sound Surround

But record buyers were looking for solace as well as catharsis, and many of them found it in the disparate worlds of soft rock and heavy metal. James Taylor's *Sweet Baby James* and Joni Mitchell's *Ladies Of The Canyon* were the dual cornerstones of the burgeoning "sensitive singer-songwriter" movement, while Bread's "Make It With You" and The Carpenters' "(They Long To Be) Close To You" filled the AM airwaves with melodic softness. On the flip side of the coin, Blue Cheer, Vanilla Fudge, and Iron Butterfly had all struck individual blows for **heavy rock** during the late sixties; but now Mountain, The Amboy Dukes, Frijid Pink, Cold Blood, The Frost, Rare Earth, Moloch, and dozens of other like-minded bands were coming out of the woodwork, cranking their amps past the threshold of physical pain, and playing simplified blues licks like there was no tomorrow. Biggest of all these bands was Michigan's indefatigable **Grand Funk Railroad**, who landed no less than three albums in the charts in a period of ten months: *Grand Funk* came in at number eleven, *Closer To Home* at number six, and *Live Album* made it all the way to number five. If their music lacked a certain subtlety, at least it was really loud and you could boogie to it.

'70 Janis Joplin

Tragic Chemistry

All of which made the death of rock's leading innovator even more tragic. Jimi Hendrix, whose approach to the electric guitar had completely revolutionized the instrument, choked to death on his own vomit on September 18th. He was twenty-seven. **Janis Joplin**, America's most popular white blues singer, was the same age when she died of a heroin overdose on October 4. Elvis Presley, no stranger to pharmaceuticals himself, was nonetheless concerned about the spread of illicit drugs in America. Or so he said in his letter to

TOP ALBUMS

SIMON AND GARFUNKEL
Bridge Over Troubled Water

CREEDENCE CLEARWATER REVIVAL
Cosmo's Factory

SANTANA
Abraxas

VARIOUS ARTISTS
Woodstock

THE BEATLES
Let It Be

President Nixon. In the year's most bizarre summit meeting, the President invited Elvis to the White House to award him a Drug Enforcement Agency badge, something that the badge-collecting Elvis had been coveting for some time. Nixon's aides mistakenly thought that Elvis might have some pull with young voters; for his part, Elvis advised Nixon that the best way to calm student unrest was to kick John Lennon out of the country.

TV News

One of Nixon's few popular moves in 1970 was signing a bill banning cigarette advertising on radio and television. Other good news for TV viewers was the introduction of three new high-quality comedy programs: the sitcoms *The Odd Couple* (starring Jack Klugman and Tony Randall) and *The Mary Tyler Moore Show*, and the variety-format *Flip Wilson Show*. The three most popular new shows among children were all about people (or animals) in rock bands: *Josie and the*

'70 The Partridge Family.

Pussycats, animated forerunners of bands like The Go-Gos and The Bangles; *Lancelot Link, Secret Chimp*, a live-action spy spoof starring a cast of chimpanzees, who also played together as The Evolution Revolution; and ***The Partridge Family***, a sitcom about a family that decided to form a rock band. In the grand tradition of The Monkees, The Partridge Family (based on real-life family pop group The Cowsills) actually had several chart hits, including "I Think I Love You" and "I'll Meet You Halfway." David Cassidy, who played the family's eldest son and lead singer, was featured regularly in teeny-bopper magazines like *16* and *Tiger Beat*.

Import Fighting Grows Ugly

As America experienced its worst recession in several years, Detroit became increasingly concerned with the growing popularity of import cars. AMC responded to the situation with the Gremlin, a tiny two-door hatchback with a base price starting below two thousand dollars. Available in various unpleasant earth tones, the Gremlin was one of the quintessentially ugly cars of the 1970s. Much better looking was Chevy's new, sportier-styled Camaro; an immediate hit with consumers, the car would later be seen every week on TV's *The Rockford Files*. Less popular was the company's import-fighting Vega; along with an unattractive exterior, the compact was notorious for oil leaks and rapid body rust.

Rearguard Action Damages Ford

Ford's Pinto was, without question, the most notorious car of the decade. The popular compact's fuel tank was mounted in such a way that left it extremely vulnerable in rear-end collisions, and the 1971–76 models were plagued by often-fatal fires and explosions. Numerous lawsuits ensued; instead of settling with the victims, Ford's lawyers fought the litigation all the way to the Supreme Court, thus severely hurting the company's reputation.

IN THE NEWS

March 11 – Timothy Leary sentenced to ten years in prison for possession of marijuana.

April 11 – *Apollo 13* mission to the Moon launched, but crippled by explosion of liquid oxygen tank. Mission makes it to Moon, orbits it and returns to Earth safely on April 17.

April 22 – Earth Day, a celebration of the Earth's ecology, is observed for the first time across the country.

April 30 – President Nixon announces the US invasion of Cambodia, directly contradicting his repeated pledges to pull US forces out of Southeast Asia.

May 4 – An anti-war rally at Kent State University in Kent, Ohio, leaves four people dead after National Guardsmen fire into crowd of 600 protesters.

May 9 – Anti-war protests erupt across the country, including a 100,000-strong demonstration in Washington DC.

June 13 – Nixon appoints a Commission on Campus Unrest to determine causes of, and possible solutions to, campus violence.

IN THE NEWS

June 15 – US Supreme Court rules that "conscientious objector" status can also apply to those opposing the Vietnam War on moral grounds.

July 4 – "Honor America Day" observed in Washington DC by thousands of people marching in support of the Nixon administration's war policies.

September 13 – Timothy Leary escapes from a minimum-security prison near San Luis Obispo, California. Leary flees to Algiers, where he joins exiled Black Panther leader Eldridge Cleaver.

October 7 – President Nixon presents five-point peace plan to North Vietnamese, who reject it.

December – US troop deaths in Vietnam War rise to 44,000.

December 21 – Reduction of minimum voting age to eighteen approved by US Supreme Court.

ACADEMY AWARDS

Best Picture

Patton

directed by Franklin Schaffner

Best Actor

George C Scott

Patton

Best Actress

Glenda Jackson

Women in Love

'70 "Love means never having to say you're sorry." O'Neal and MacGraw star in *Love Story*.

Movie News

Paul Newman (*WUSA*) and Barbra Streisand (*On a Clear Day You Can See Forever, The Owl and the Pussycat*) were the year's most popular movie stars, but audiences also flocked to see George C Scott command a tank battalion in *Patton*, Dustin Hoffman age a century in *Little Big Man*, and Jack Nicholson order a chicken salad sandwich in *Five Easy Pieces*.

The decidedly anti-war *M*A*S*H* starred Donald Sutherland and Elliott Gould as a pair of irreverent US Army surgeons serving in the Korean War. ***Airport***, based on Arthur Hailey's best-selling novel about a plane in peril, started the vogue for all-star cast disaster movies that would last through the end of the decade. Written by future film critic Roger Ebert, *Beyond the Valley of the Dolls* was Russ Meyer's raunchy morality tale about an all-girl rock band trying to make it to the top—and with everyone in sight.

But the year's biggest smash was ***Love Story***, based on Erich Segal's best-selling novel. Ryan O'Neal and Ali MacGraw were perfectly cast as the film's tragic lovers; O'Neal was nominated for an Academy Award for his performance, and MacGraw instantly became one of the most sought-after actresses in America.

Some Positions Examined

America's struggle to come to terms with the thorny issues of sexual revolution and women's liberation was reflected by the best-selling books lists. Dr David Reuben's *Everything You Always Wanted to Know About Sex*, J's *The Sensuous Woman*, Kate Millet's *Sexual Politics*, and Dr William H Masters and Virginia Johnson's *Human Sexual Inadequacy* were some of the books taking up residency on the country's nightstands. Also popular, on a more underground level, were Jerry Rubin's *Do It!* (billed as "The most important political statement made by a white revolutionary in America today"), and *Soledad Brother*, a collection of George Jackson's prison writings. Jackson, serving a sentence for murdering a prison guard, was killed while trying to escape San Quentin in August 1971.

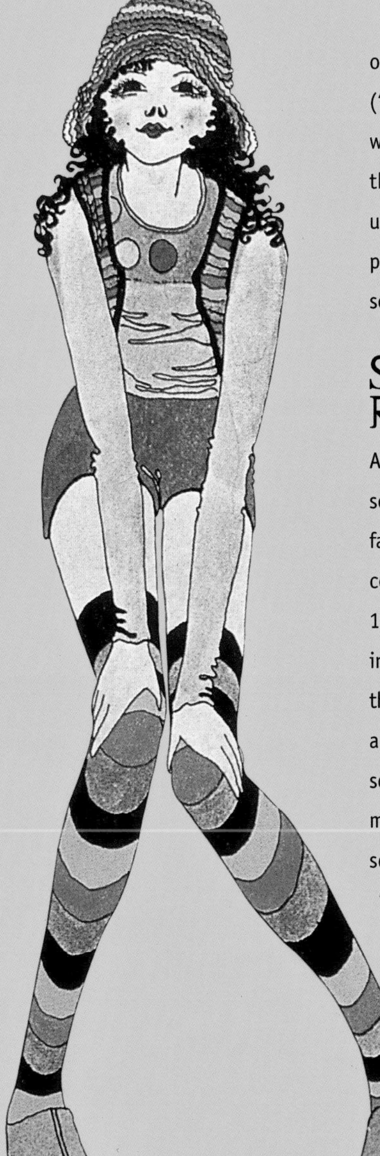

Tie-Dyed And Earth Bound

Fashion in 1970 seemed to have little rhyme or reason; while both sexes were wearing tie-dyed shirts, "unisex" bell-bottoms and second-hand military attire (for an ironic-yet-stylish comment on the Vietnam War), women were also wearing mid-calf hemlines, granny dresses, and "hot pants." The latter, an even shorter update of the previous decade's "short-shorts," were often made from suede or velvet and sewn with colorful patches.

"Earth shoes," designed so that one's heel sits lower than one's toe ("the way your feet were born to walk," according to the ads) became all the rage, despite being horribly unattractive. On the other hand, platform shoes were starting to make serious inroads with the "glam" set.

Search And Rescue

As the decade began, the search for self-awareness—a subject of much fascination in underground and collegiate circles since The Beatles' 1967 visit to India—became an increasingly mainstream concept. After the rampant consumerism of the fifties and early sixties, and the tremendous social upheavals of the last few years, many Americans believed that the solutions to their problems lay in "finding themselves;" as a result, many **self-help movements**, from Werner Erhard's EST to Transcendental Meditation (or "TM"), became extremely trendy.

'70 Hot pants. Hmmm...

nineteen 71

As seekers of spiritual enlightenment began to explore various forms of Native American mysticism, the early seventies gave rise to increasing public awareness of Native American history and culture. In 1971, Dee Brown published *Bury My Heart at Wounded Knee,* a meticulously researched and deeply depressing account of the US government's genocidal nineteenth-century campaign against the American Indians.

TOP TELEVISION SHOWS

- ***The Flip Wilson Show***
- ***Marcus Welby, MD***
- ***Gunsmoke***
- ***All in the Family***
- ***Sanford and Son***

Now also on the wrong end of the government's rifles, many young people began to realize that the "Cowboys good, Indians bad" attitude drummed into them by countless westerns might actually have been a gross over-simplification. One famous pro-ecology commercial even featured Indian actor Iron Eyes Cody shedding a tear over America's trash-strewn landscape.

On June 11, a group of American Indians ended their nineteen-month occupation of Alcatraz Island in San Francisco. The fifteen protesters, who were forcibly removed by US marshals, had claimed the island under a provision in a treaty between the US and the Indian nations which gave American Indians free run of unused federal lands.

Chart Topical

Native American consciousness made it into the pop charts as well, courtesy of The Raiders' "Indian Reservation." Originally recorded by English vocalist Don Fardon, the song presented the plight of modern Native Americans in an empathetic, straightforward manner. Social commentary continued to be a viable way to have a hit record, as proved by The Undisputed Truth's "Smiling Faces Sometimes," The Chi-Lites' "(For God's Sake) Give More Power To The People," and Freda Payne's anti-war anthem, "Bring The Boys Home." Even Cher's melodramatic "Gypsies, Tramps And Thieves," her first major hit since 1967, dealt with the still-topical issue of racial prejudice.

Family Fortunes

There was still plenty of room on the charts for good clean fun, however. The Jackson Five, a group of brothers from Gary, Indiana, continued their chart dominance (they'd already scored four Number One singles between 1969 and 1970) with "Mama's Pearl," "Never Can Say Goodbye," and "Sugar Daddy", while thirteen-year-old lead vocalist Michael even stepped out for a solo smash, "Got To Be There." The Osmonds, another of the year's top acts, were like a white, Mormon version of The Jackson Five; while the band had hits with "One Bad Apple," "Double Lovin'," and "Yo-Yo," teen heartthrob Donny had hits of his own with "Go Away Little Girl," "Sweet And Innocent," and "Hey Girl."

Alice Cooper (real name Vincent Furnier) stepped to the forefront of the rock scene; notorious for outrageous onstage antics (he was even rumored to have slaughtered chickens during a concert), Alice and his band actually produced two of the best hard-rock records of the year, *Love It To Death* and *Killer*. Frightening on a much deeper level was Sly and The Family Stone's *There's A Riot Goin' On*, which viewed the current American malaise through a cocaine-laced veil of paranoia. *Shaft*, Isaac Hayes' wah-wah-fueled soundtrack to the popular film about a bad mutha ("Shut yo'

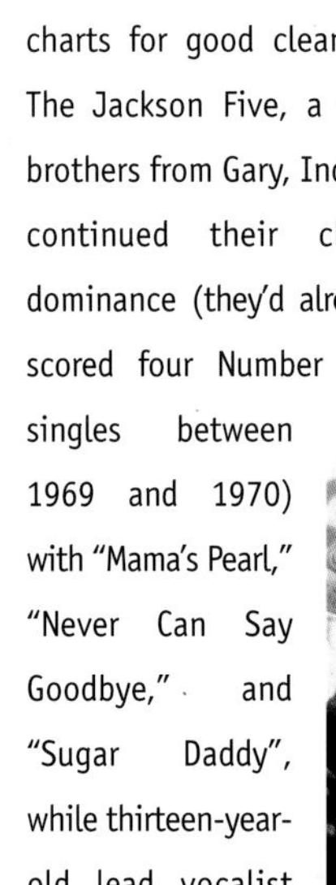

'71 The Jackson Five.

mouth"), set the musical tone for the "blaxploitation" scores of the next half-decade.

James Taylor and Joni Mitchell were back, with *Mudslide Slim and The Blue Horizon* and *Blue*, respectively, but the light-a-candle-and-have-a-good-cry album of the year honors truly belonged to Carole King's ***Tapestry***. At a time when everyone was still trying to come to terms with the radical changes of the last five years, songs like "It's Too Late" and "So Far Away" hit the zeitgeist square on the forehead, and kept *Tapestry* at the top of the album charts for nearly five months.

Doors vocalist Jim Morrison, aged twenty-seven, died of a heart attack in Paris on July 3; he was followed three days later by Louis "Satchmo" Armstrong, whose gravelly voice made him even more famous than his superb trumpet playing. Duane Allman, the promising guitarist for The Allman Brothers Band, died October 29 in a motorcycle accident, aged twenty-four. Many also shed tears when Bill Graham announced the closing of his Fillmore East and West ballrooms; the venues, which were the hip places to play in New York City and San Francisco during the late sixties, had been hemorrhaging money for years.

Creative Accounts

Though the continuing recession caused many of the major film studios to tighten their budgets, the belt-tightening didn't really seem to hurt the quality of their projects. William Friedkin's *The French Connection*, Robert Altman's *McCabe And Mrs. Miller*, Alan J Pakula's *Klute*, Peter Bogdanovich's *The Last Picture Show*, Samuel Peckinpah's *Straw Dogs*, and Monte Hellman's *Two Lane Blacktop* all relied on excellent direction, good stories and en-gagingly complex characters rather than big budgets, and yet (with the exception of *Two Lane Blacktop*) all of them still made money at the box office.

1971 was also the year that "blaxploitation" films—action-themed pictures geared towards black audiences—began to appear regularly

'71 Alice Cooper.

TOP SINGLES

Three Dog Night
"Joy To The World"

Rod Stewart
"Maggie May"

Carole King
"It's Too Late"

The Osmonds
"One Bad Apple"

The Bee Gees
"How Can You Mend A Broken Heart"

IN THE NEWS

April 23 – Numerous Vietnam veterans return their medals and decorations as part of an anti-war protest in Washington DC.

May 3 – Anti-war demonstrators attempt to stop government activities by blocking traffic into Washington DC during the morning rush hour.

May 30 – US spacecraft *Mariner 9* achieves a successful orbit of Mars.

June 13 – The first installment of "The Pentagon Papers"—excerpts taken from the Pentagon's classified study, *History of the US Decision-Making Process on Vietnam Policy*—is published in *The New York Times*. Former Defense Department analyst Daniel Ellsberg admits to leaking the material to the *Times*, and is indicted for theft and possession of secret documents.

September 9–13 – 43 people die in riots at Attica State correctional Facility in Attica, NY.

November 24 – Somewhere between Seattle, Washington and Reno, Nevada, hijacker DB Cooper parachutes from a Northwest Orient jet with $200,000 in ransom money. Cooper, who is never apprehended, becomes an instant folk hero.

December 26 – The heaviest bombing of North Vietnam since November 1968 commences.

in theaters, led by Gordon Parks' *Shaft* and Melvin Van Peebles' *Sweet Sweetback's Baad Asssss Song*. *Billy Jack*, starring Tom Laughlin (who also wrote and directed) as a karate expert who faces off against "The Man," was

'71 Peter Falk as Columbo.

ACADEMY AWARDS

Best Picture

The French Connection

directed by William Friedkin

Best Actress

Jane Fonda

Klute

Best Actor

Gene Hackman

The French Connection

Rod Stewart

Every Picture Tells A Story

another massive low-budget hit. Pricier, but just as silly, was Boris Sagal's *The Omega Man*; as the last living man in Los Angeles, Charlton Heston fought off an army of zombies, grimaced meaningfully and watched endless screenings of *Woodstock*. Watch out for the brown acid, Chuck!

TV News

In the grand tradition of Milton Berle, American viewers tuned in every week to see **Flip Wilson** dress up in drag. His female character, Geraldine, was *The Flip Wilson Show*'s most popular feature; her signature lines, "What you see is what you get!" and "The Devil made me do it!" became two of the year's most oft-uttered catch-phrases. People tuned in to ***All in the Family*** for very different reasons; as the bigoted, lower-middle-class dock worker Archie Bunker, Carroll O'Connor played a character that appealed as much to those who laughed at his ignorance, as it did to those who shared his discomfort with the rapidly changing world around them.

Sanford and Son, an all-black adaptation of the popular British show *Steptoe and Son*, was almost as popular as *All in the Family*, and received almost as much criticism; many viewers felt that Redd Foxx's portrayal of a lazy, scheming junkman Fred Sanford (and Whitman Mayo's portrayal of Grady, Fred's wine-headed pal) only perpetuated **stereotypes** about black people. No complaints were made about the stereotypes of fat people perpetuated by *Cannon*, even though William Conrad's portly private eye was often seen helping himself to the delicacies of whatever locale he happened to be investigating.

Featured as a regular installment of *The NBC Mystery Movie*, ***Columbo*** (with Peter Falk in the title role) was one of television's more popular detectives. Decked out in a ratty raincoat and wrinkled suit, Columbo's mind was as sharp as his appearance was disheveled; half the fun of the show was seeing him toy with criminals who almost never took him seriously. Clothes, or the lack thereof, were a big part of *The Sonny and Cher Comedy Hour*'s appeal, as viewers regularly tuned in to see what **Cher** would (or wouldn't) be wearing. Originally introduced as a summer-replacement variety show, the highly rated series gave the duo's career a new lease of life.

Smiley All The Way To The Bank

Manhattan button manufacturer NG Slater brought out his new line of yellow "smiley-face" buttons in 1969, but nobody seemed to want them. Perhaps it was increasing unemployment rates, or maybe people were just looking for an alternative to the ubiquitous peace sign, but in 1971, the buttons suddenly started to sell like crazy. Twenty million of the "Have a nice day" pin (as they became known) were sold in six months, ensuring that Slater would indeed have numerous nice days to come.

Disney's Plot

Walt Disney World opened in Florida, on a 27,500-acre site. The Disney company had spent years buying up lots in and around Orlando, hoping to avoid the buildup of motels like the ones that ringed their Anaheim park. The two parks themselves were similar in terms of rides and attractions, although Disney World's would eventually enable the park to accommodate the Epcot Center.

'71 Sonny and Cher take off on prime-time TV.

TOP ALBUMS

Carole King

Tapestry

Janis Joplin

Pearl

George Harrison

All Things Must Pass

Santana

Santana III

Rod Stewart

Every Picture Tells A Story

nineteen 72

In the wake of the Kent State shootings, and with the Vietnam War still raging, it was a matter of some debate as to whether Richard Nixon (and Spiro Agnew, his loose cannon of a vice-president) would actually be re-elected in November. But "Tricky Dickie," as his detractors called him, proved to be extremely resourceful when the chips (and his approval ratings) were down.

TOP TELEVISION SHOWS

All in the Family
Sanford And Son
The Flip Wilson Show
Hawaii Five-O
The Mary Tyler Moore Show

ACADEMY AWARDS

Best Picture
The Godfather
directed by Francis Ford Coppola

Best Actor
Marlon Brando
The Godfather

Best Actress
Liza Minnelli
Cabaret

Foreign policy was always Nixon's strong suit, and his historic visits to China and Russia not only improved relations between the US and those countries, but substantially boosted his popularity back home.

Though rumors of his administration's involvement in the Watergate affair continued to surface, Nixon received some unwitting help in the election from his Democratic opponent, Senator **George McGovern**. McGovern's original running mate, Senator Thomas Eagleton, was forced to withdraw from the race on July 31, when evidence surfaced that he had received psychiatric treatment for nervous exhaustion during the early sixties. McGovern's indecision over whether or not to stand by his man (R Sargent Shriver, the former head of the Peace Corps, took Eagleton's place in August) severely hampered his campaign's momentum; in addition, many moderate and conservative voters were put off by his proposal of amnesty for draft-dodgers. On November 5, Secretary of State Henry Kissinger's casual hint of an impending Vietnam peace settlement sealed McGovern's fate; two days later, Nixon was re-elected with 60.7 percent of the popular vote.

Ms-Information

The burgeoning strength of the Women's Liberation movement was reflected in the US Senate's passing of the Equal Rights Amendment, which prohibited discrimination on the basis of sex. The amendment was then sent to the individual states for ratification; by the end of the year, twenty-two of the required thirty-eight states had ratified it.

Ms magazine, a monthly periodical edited by noted feminist Gloria Steinem, first appeared in 1972. Radically different from such popular female-oriented publications as *Redbook* and *Good Housekeeping*, *Ms*, according to Steinem, wouldn't tell you "how to make jelly, but how to seize control of your life."

Movie News

Superfly, directed Gordon Parks, Jr (the son of the man who directed *Shaft*), starred Ron O' Neal as a nattily attired coke dealer looking to make one last big score before getting out of the business. In addition to further fanning the flames of the "blaxploitation" fad (1972 also produced Barry Shear's *Across 110th Street* and William Crain's *Blacula*), the film presaged the infiltration of **cocaine** and flashy "pimp" clothes (platform shoes, flare-collared shirts, wide-lapelled suits) into the American mainstream. *Dirty Harry*, Don Seigel's fast-moving drama about a rule-breaking cop, turned journeyman actor **Clint Eastwood** into a film icon, and his "Feel lucky, punk?" line into a popular catchphrase. Burt Reynolds also saw his career take off in 1972; he received critical raves for his adrenalized performance in John Boorman's *Deliverance*, but it was a nude spread in the April issue of *Cosmopolitan* that really increased his popularity.

Women In The Spotlight

Marlon Brando, whose career had taken an erratic turn during the past decade, gave a memorable performance as Don Vito Corleone in Francis Ford Coppola's *The Godfather*. Even more memorable, for Academy Award viewers, was the sight of Sacheen Littlefeather, dressed in traditional Apache garb, stepping to the podium to accept Brando's *Godfather* Oscar. Ms Littlefeather, President of the National Native American Affirmative Image Committee, was allowed to read only a short excerpt from Brando's fifteen-page acceptance speech.

Barbra Streisand (*What's Up, Doc?* and *Up the Sandbox*) was the year's most popular female

TOP SINGLES

Roberta Flack
"The First Time Ever I Saw Your Face"

Gilbert O' Sullivan
"Alone Again (Naturally)"

Don McLean
"American Pie"

Nilsson
"Without You"

Johnny Nash
"I Can See Clearly Now"

star, and Liza Minnelli and Diana Ross received raves for their turns in *Cabaret* and *Lady Sings the Blues*, but **Jane Fonda** received far more press—good and bad—than all of them put together. In protest at the Vietnam War, Fonda visited Hanoi and posed for pictures with a North Vietnamese anti-aircraft gun, a move which alienated her from many citizens and GIs. Even in the 1990s, long after she had settled into ruling-class respectability as the wife of broadcasting mogul Ted Turner, bumper stickers reading "Boycott Jane Fonda, America's Traitor Bitch" could still be seen on the occasional passing car.

Deep Blue

Linda Lovelace also received plenty of notoriety for her performance in *Deep Throat*, the first hardcore porn film to be released in commercial movie houses. Lovelace cheerfully made the rounds on the talk-show circuit (and even showed up at the Academy Awards) to promote the film, which ushered in a brief period where porn flicks were treated with the same curiousity and respect afforded to French art films. Years later, she published a book claiming she was forced into the porn business by her abusive husband/manager.

TV News

Maude, an offshoot of *All in the Family*, featured Bea Arthur as a voluble feminist, and *M*A*S*H** (starring Alan Alda as Army surgeon Hawkeye Pierce) continued in the anti-war vein of its filmic namesake; the popularity of both shows proved that programs with pronounced liberal themes could still be successful. Nothing beat good old-fashioned family values, something ***The Waltons***, a heartwarming series about a rural family living in the Depression era, had by the wagonload. ***The Bob Newhart Show***, another popular new show, was a well-crafted comedy whose basic premise—a psychiatrist and his group of eccentric patients—was tailor-made for Newhart's deadpan brand of humor. One of the year's surprise hits was *Emergency!*, an hour-long, multi-vignette drama that followed events at a Los Angeles hospital as well as a neighboring fire department. *The Rookies*, an early Aaron Spelling production about three new police recruits, also did well with viewers, although the show was one of many criticized for **excessive violence**. When the US Surgeon General released a study claiming that TV violence had little effect on children, it was widely slammed as slanted in favor of the TV industry.

IN THE NEWS

February 5 – Due to increased airplane hijackings, the screening of passengers and luggage becomes mandatory on all domestic and foreign flights by US airlines.

February 21–28 – President Nixon makes a historic visit to China, in which the two nations agree to work to lessen risk of war, to normalize relations, and to increase scientific and cultural ties.

April 16 – *Apollo 16* launched; astronauts Charles Duke and Thomas K Mattingly walk on Moon's surface on April 20, conducting tests and collecting rocks.

May 15 – Alabama Governor George Wallace shot while campaigning for the presidency in Laurel, Maryland. The assassination attempt leaves Wallace paralyzed from the waist down.

May 22–30 – Nixon travels to Moscow, the first visit by a US president in history.

June 4 – Black activist Angela Davis is found innocent of abetting a 1970 courtroom escape that left four dead.

June 17 – Police arrest five men for breaking into the Democratic Party headquarters in the Watergate apartment complex in Washington DC. One of them is James McCord, a former CIA agent currently working for the Republican National Committee and the Committee to Re-elect the president. Democratic Party chief Larry O'Brien charges Nixon's campaign staff with "political espionage."

July 10–14 – Democratic National Convention nominates Senator George McGovern for president. McGovern vows to end the Vietnam War within 90 days of taking office.

Music News

AM radio was still king of the airwaves in 1972, embracing a wide cross-section of material that included soul (The Chi-Lites' "Oh Girl," Billy Paul's "Me and Mrs Jones"), soft rock (America, Don McLean), full-on schmaltz (Sammy Davis, Jr's "The Candy Man," Neil Diamond's "Song Sung Blue"), and novelty discs (Hot Butter's Moog opus "Popcorn," The Jimmy Castor Bunch's "Troglodyte"). Helen Reddy hit Number One with her feminist anthem "I Am Woman," while Michael Jackson topped the charts with "Ben," the lovely title song from a gory film about a killer rat.

Soul and funk music was growing in leaps and bounds, with the innovative arrangements of The Temptations' "Papa Was A Rollin' Stone," The O'Jays' "Backstabbers," and The Dramatics' "In The Rain" leading the way. **James Brown**, the hardest-working man in show business, paused between his successful "Talking Loud And Saying Nothing" and "Get On The Good Foot" singles to deliver the earnest anti-smack recitation, "King Heroin," which also made the Top Forty. Stevie Wonder's *Talking Book* and Curtis Mayfield's *Superfly* were two of 1972's finest albums; the former featured "Superstition" and "You Are The Sunshine of My Life," while the latter provided the funky soundtrack to one of the year's most popular movies.

VD Catches On

With the economy at its healthiest since 1967, unemployment and inflation were way down from the previous year. The same could not be said for sexually transmitted diseases, however; according to Federal health officials, some 2,300,000 new cases of gonorrhea were reported in 1972, as well as a hundred thousand new cases of infectious syphillis, the biggest increase for either disease since the introduction of antibiotics. As many Americans participating in the "**sexual revolution**" were woefully uninformed about venereal disease, a series of "VD is for Everybody" public-service television ads were put into regular rotation on televison. Across the nation, confused children looked up from the family TV set and asked, "Mom, what's VD?"

The Denim Decade

Just when you thought that AMC's Gremlin couldn't get any uglier, the company attempted to capitalize on America's current infatuation with denim by introducing the "Levi's Edition" Gremlin, which came complete with copper rivets and denim-like blue nylon on the seats and door panels. Much easier on the eyes were the 1973 Lincoln Continentals, the first Continentals to be manufactured with padded vinyl roofs and oval "opera" windows. Lincoln stayed true to the popular look through the end of the decade.

Going For Gold

1972 produced American heroes in two unlikely sports. In Munich, swimmer Mark Spitz set an Olympic record by winning seven gold medals at the 1972 Summer Olympics, and was immediately deluged by offers of endorsements and movie roles. In Reykjavik, Iceland, **Bobby Fischer** became the first American to win the World Chess Championship, beating the USSR's Boris Spassky for the title. In the wake of his victory, retailers reported record sales of chess sets.

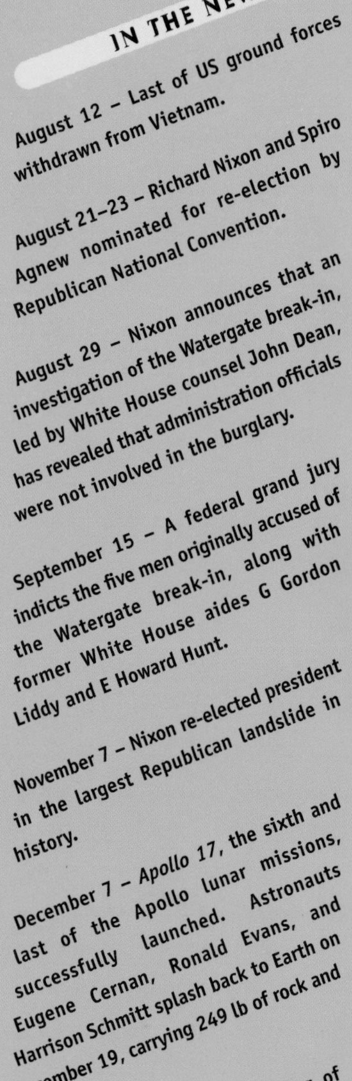

IN THE NEWS

August 12 – Last of US ground forces withdrawn from Vietnam.

August 21–23 – Richard Nixon and Spiro Agnew nominated for re-election by Republican National Convention.

August 29 – Nixon announces that an investigation of the Watergate break-in, led by White House counsel John Dean, has revealed that administration officials were not involved in the burglary.

September 15 – A federal grand jury indicts the five men originally accused of the Watergate break-in, along with former White House aides G Gordon Liddy and E Howard Hunt.

November 7 – Nixon re-elected president in the largest Republican landslide in history.

December 7 – *Apollo 17*, the sixth and last of the Apollo lunar missions, successfully launched. Astronauts Eugene Cernan, Ronald Evans, and Harrison Schmitt splash back to Earth on December 19, carrying 249 lb of rock and soil samples.

December 18 – Full-scale bombing of North Vietnam resumes after Paris peace negotiations reach impasse. The bombings are halted again on December 30.

TOP ALBUMS

Chicago
Chicago V

Don McLean
American Pie

Elton John
Honkey Chateau

Roberta Flack
First Take

America
America

'72 Olympic champion Mark Spitz.

nineteen 73

The draft had been ended, and the war in Vietnam was finally drawing to a close, but America was in no mood to celebrate. Everywhere you turned, there was unsettling news. In California, for example, Juan Corona was sentenced to twenty-five consecutive life terms for the 1971 murders of twenty-five migrant workers.

ACADEMY AWARDS

Best Picture
The Sting
directed by George Roy Hill

Best Actor
Jack Lemmon
Save the Tiger

Best Actress
Glenda Jackson
A Touch of Class

TOP TELEVISION SHOWS

All in the Family
The Waltons
Sanford and Son
Hawaii Five-O
Maude

In Wounded Knee, South Dakota, armed members of the militant American Indian Movement held Federal forces at bay while calling for the free election of tribal officials, the investigation of the Bureau of Indian Affairs, and a review of all US–Indian treaties. There were endless lines at gas stations, thanks to the OPEC oil embargo, and nationwide meat boycotts resulting from inflated hamburger prices.

More troubling were the continued rumblings about the **Watergate** break-in, and the growing suspicion that the Nixon administration was unbelievably corrupt. Under sworn testimony, John Dean stunned the country with revelations of the White House "enemies list," a running tally of people targeted for IRS and FBI harassment because of their opposition (real or imagined) to the Nixon administration. On November 17, Nixon remarked to the Associated Press Managing Editors Convention: "People have the right to know whether or not their president is a crook. Well, I am not a crook." But as the House of Representatives busied itself preparing eight impeachment resolutions, it was looking increasingly as if nobody believed him.

Movie News

Given the downcast state of the nation, the success of period films like *Paper Moon* and *The Sting* made perfect sense; people were looking to escape to another time and place, and the simpler, the better. George Lucas' *American Graffiti*, with its big cars, teenage traumas, and soundtrack of rock 'n' roll classics from the late fifties and early sixties, provided a bittersweet snaphot of a time only ten years past, yet seemingly centuries away. Martin Scorsese made a name for himself with *Mean Streets*, a memorably intense film about two-bit hoods in New York's Little Italy, starring little-known actors Harvey Keitel and **Robert De Niro**; De Niro also starred in *Bang The Drum Slowly*, John Hancock's moving portrait of a baseball player dying of leukemia. Almost as gritty and exciting as Scorsese's film was *Serpico*, starring Al Pacino as a cop battling corruption in his own department, and *The Harder They Come*, a Jamaican film about a criminal who becomes a reggae idol. The latter film made an international singing star out of Jimmy Cliff, and went a long way towards popularizing reggae music in America.

'73 ***American Graffiti*** **captured the spirit of 1962—and grossed $55 million.**

Science And Religion On Film

Westworld (about robotic rebellion at a fantasy resort) and *Soylent Green* (in which the US government solves the overpopulation problem by turning corpses into food) were the year's two most popular science fiction flicks, while the filmic adaptations of popular God-rock musicals *Godspell* and *Jesus Christ Superstar* provoked endless arguments about who was the better Jesus, Victor Garber or Ted Neeley.

'73 Al Pacino in *Serpico*.

But, for the most part, if moviegoers weren't lining up to see Marlon Brando butter up Maria Schneider in Bernardo Bertolucci's *Last Tango in Paris*, they were plunking down money to see Linda Blair vomit pea soup in William Friedkin's ***The Exorcist***. Blair became famous overnight as the twelve-year-old girl possessed by the devil, even though Mercedes McCambridge (voice) and Eileen Smith (body) deputized for her during the possession scenes (both actresses had to sue to get screen credit). In any case, the truly frightening film made more money than any horror movie before it.

Dragon Exits

After many years as a star in Hong Kong martial-arts films, Bruce Lee had finally broken through to the US mainstream (thanks to films like *Fists of Fury* and *The Chinese Connection*) when he died mysteriously of a brain edema at the age of thirty-two. *Enter The Dragon*, his final complete film, was a box-office smash.

Rock On The Box

Americans watched a lot of Watergate coverage in 1973; from May 17 to November 17, the three networks split live broadcasts of the hearings during the day, while PBS aired taped highlights in the evenings. Education of a cheerier note was provided by *Schoolhouse Rock*, three-minute educational cartoons broadcast during ABS's Saturday morning programming. The musical segments included "Multiplication Rock," "Grammar Rock", "America Rock," and "Science Rock," all of which proved remarkably effective as learning tools; today, you'd be hard-pressed to find an American adult between the ages of twenty-five and thirty-five who doesn't remember songs like "Three is a Magic Number," "A Noun Is A Person, Place Or Thing," or "Sufferin' Until Sufferage."

Equally instructive, in its own depressing way, was Elvis Presley's *Elvis:* ***Aloha From Hawaii***; broadcast to over one and a half billion viewers in forty different countries on April 4, the concert showed what happens when a man

IN THE NEWS

January 22 – Vietnam peace agreement signed in Paris by representatives of the US, South Vietnam and the Viet Cong.

January 30 – James W McCord and G Gordon Liddy convicted of breaking into and illegally wiretapping Democratic Party headquarters at the Watergate apartment complex.

March 23 – Watergate Judge John J Sirica publicizes a letter written to him by James W McCord, which claims that Nixon Administration officials had applied political pressure to him and other defendants to plead guilty and keep quiet about the break-in.

April 27 – Acting FBI director L Patrick Gray resigns after revelations surface that he had intentionally destroyed records involving the Watergate break-in.

May 14 – The *Skylab* station is successfully launched into Earth orbit, although its solar panels are damaged during the launch.

May 17 – The Senate Select Committee on Presidential Campaign Activities, headed by North Carolina Senator Sam Ervin, opens televised hearings to explore the alleged cover-up of the Nixon administration's involvement in the Watergate affair.

May 25 – *Skylab 2* carries astronauts Charles Conrad, Joseph Kerwin and Paul Weitz to rendevouz with *Skylab* station. The three repair solar panels and conduct scientific experiments, before returning to Earth on June 22.

June 16–25 – USSR Party Secretary Leonid I Brezhnev visits US.

believes his own press and eats too many double cheeseburgers. Just four and a half years after his remarkable "Comeback Special," The King looked haggard and overweight as he sleepwalked through classics like "Hound Dog" and "Blue Suede Shoes," but his notoriously forgiving fans still sent the soundtrack from the broadcast to the top of the album charts.

After *Kojak* made him a superstar, **Telly Savalas** also tried his hand at recording, but albums like *Who Loves Ya, Baby?* and *Telly Like It Is* weren't nearly as memorable as the wise-cracking, lollipop-sucking (a substitute for cigarettes, you see) New York cop he played on TV. Buddy Ebsen, an old song-and-dance man himself, came back from *Beverly Hillbillies* purgatory as the titular mild-mannered, milk-drinking detective on *Barnaby Jones*.

An American Family, Craig Gilbert's twelve-week PBS documentary about the Loud family of Santa Barbara, California, anticipated MTV's *Real World* by a good twenty years. Edited down from three hundred hours of footage, the controversial program is best remembered for the episode in which teenaged son Lance comes out.

'73 Telly Savalas.

TOP SINGLES

Roberta Flack
"Killing Me Softly With His Song"

Dawn, featuring Tony Orlando
"Tie A Yellow Ribbon Round The Ole Oak Tree"

Paul McCartney and Wings
"My Love"

Carly Simon
"You're So Vain"

Elton John
"Crocodile Rock"

IN THE NEWS

June 25–29 – White House counsel John Dean testifies before the Senate Watergate Committee, implicating himself, White House Chief of Staff HR Haldeman, Assistant of Domestic Affairs John Erlichman, former Attorney General John Mitchell, and President Richard Nixon in the Watergate cover-up.

July 16 – Former White House aide Alexander Butterfield reveals the existence of secret recordings Nixon made of White House conversations. Though subpoenaed for them by special prosecutor Archibald Cox, Nixon refuses to release them.

July 28 – *Skylab 3* makes a rendezvous with the orbiting *Skylab* station; astronauts Alan Bean, Owen Garriott, and Jack Lousma perform further repairs and experiments.

September 4 – John Erlichman and G Gordon Liddy indicted in connection with the burglary of the office of Daniel Ellsberg's psychiatrist; following Ellsberg's leak of the "Pentagon Papers," the two were allegedly looking for evidence that would link Ellsburg to the KGB.

Pop At A Low Ebb

1973 was, quite frankly, a rather dire year for American music. The New York Dolls recorded their legendary first album, and Iggy Pop and The Stooges released *Raw Power*. However, most Americans ignored them in favor of novelties like Tony Orlando and Dawn's "Tie a Yellow Ribbon Round The Ole Oak Tree" or sappy pop songs like Maureen McGovern's "The Morning After," the theme from the previous year's flipped-ship disaster flick *The Poseidon Adventure*. The Watkins Glen Music Festival, the last big Woodstock-style festival for several years, drew five hundred thousand people to see The Allman Brothers Band, The Grateful Dead, and The Band, but none of the performers played particularly memorable sets.

Sole Saviors

Soul music was once again radio's saving grace, with Gladys Knight and The Pips and former Temptation Eddie Kendricks scoring back-to-back Number Ones with "Midnight Train to Georgia" and "Keep On Truckin'," respectively, and The Isley Brothers offering up a sweet summer hit in "That Lady." Marvin Gaye's "Let's Get It On," The O'Jays' "Love Train," and Billy Preston's "Will It Go Round In Circles" all also topped the charts during the year, while War came close with the Latin funk of "The Cisco Kid" and "Gypsy Man." ***Soul Train***, a black version of *American Bandstand* hosted by the impossibly smooth Don Cornelius, became *the* TV show to watch for black (and white) kids interested in the latest steps, sounds and threads.

Bach Bores, But Sex Scores

Richard Bach's *Jonathan Livingston Seagull*, an existential fable about an individualistic seagull, continued to top the book best-seller lists for the second year running, although it was tough to decide which was more boring—the book, Hall Bartlett's film of it, or Neil Diamond's meandering score for the film. Alex Comfort's ***The Joy of Sex*** was much more exciting and enlightening, and became *the* sex manual of choice for liberated seventies couples. The book's runaway success inspired a 1974 the imaginatively titled *More Joy of Sex*. Oh, and in case you were still wondering, the American Psychiatric Association boldly reversed its one-hundred year stance and announced that homosexuality was not in fact a mental illness.

Game, Set, And Match

In sports, George Foreman beat Joe Frazier for the World Heavyweight boxing title, while the nationally televised "Battle of the Sexes" saw tennis champ Billie Jean King beat Bobby Riggs in three straight sets at the Houston astrodome.

In football, **OJ Simpson** set a seasonal record for rushing yardage (2,003 yards); movie roles and product endorsements (including the ad for Dingo boots, *below*) followed in quick succession.

O.J. DINGO

Glassy Smooth

A skateboard boom again swept the nation's sidewalks and parking lots, as newly introduced urethane wheels and fiberglass boards enabled skaters to enjoy a faster, safer ride.

Loungin' Around

The "leisure suit," a loose-tailored suit with flat jacket pockets, experienced a brief popularity as an after-work outfit. Often made from textured polyester blends and offered in distinctly non-professional colors like lemon yellow and robin's egg blue, leisure suits quickly became recognized as the mark of a lounge lizard, especially when worn with the winning combination of a half-unbuttoned shirt and a gold medallion. Hey, baby, want to swing?

IN THE NEWS

October 10 – Spiro Agnew pleads no contest to income tax evasion, and resigns Vice-Presidency.

October 19 – Nixon offers summary of Watergates tapes in exchange for no further inquiries. Cox refuses.

October 20 – Attorney General Elliot Richardson resigns, as does Deputy Attorney General William Ruckelshaus, after refusing Nixon's orders to fire Cox. Solicitor General Robert Bork is promoted to Acting Attorney General, and fires Cox. The incident becomes known as the "Saturday Night Massacre."

November 1 – Nixon appoints Leon Jaworski special Watergate prosecutor.

November 21 – A released White House tape is revealed to have had eighteen minutes erased from it.

December 6 – Representative Gerald R Ford sworn in as vice-president.

TOP ALBUMS

Elton John
Goodbye Yellow Brick Road

The Allman Brothers Band
Brothers and Sisters

Carly Simon
No Secrets

Chicago
Chicago VI

George Harrison
Living In The Material World

nineteen 74

TOP TELEVISION SHOWS

All in the Family
Sanford and Son
*M*A*S*H*
The Waltons
The Sonny and Cher Comedy Hour

Unless you were actually there, it's hard to imagine just how utterly loathed and reviled Richard Nixon was in the America of 1974. "Impeach Nixon" bumper stickers and placards were everywhere you turned. On playgrounds across the country, schoolchildren sang obscene songs about him. Accompanied by the appropriate combination of clenched eyebrows and jowly frown, the declaration of "I am not a crook!" was an unfailing laugh-getter at fondue parties, regardless of political persuasion.

ACADEMY AWARDS

Best Picture
The Godfather Part II
directed by Francis Ford Coppola

Best Actor
Art Carney
Harry and Tonto

Best Actress
Ellen Burstyn
Alice Doesn't Live Here Anymore

'74 Following his resignation, Richard Nixon says goodbye to his White House staff.

Nixon's "stonewalling" strategy—a carefully plotted series of public denials (given the sublimely Orwellian name of "Operation Candor" by White House strategists) and continued refusals to comply with requests for the Watergate tapes—only made things worse for him, although it's unlikely that anything could have improved his public image, short of stripping naked and **streaking** across the White House lawn. Hell, everyone else seemed to be doing it; from college campuses to downtown financial districts, Americans everywhere were shedding their clothes and going for a quick run. "The Streak," Ray Stevens' top-selling novelty single, served as a rallying cry, and the sudden appearance of various streakers lent a touch of absurdity to live performances by pianist Van Cliburn and dancer Rudolf Nureyev, *The Tonight Show*, and even the Academy Awards telecast.

Stripped To Essentials

Nudism was growing increasingly popular, spreading—much to the displeasure of local authorities—from the time-honored "nudist camps" to public beaches. Not that sunbathers within the legal limit of the law were wearing much, either; the **string bikini**, originally introduced in Rio, was now a fairly common sight on US beaches, as were men's French-cut bikini trunks. All you needed was a puka shell necklace, and your stylish beachgoing outfit was complete.

Monster Gas Guzzlers

American automobile sales were down twenty percent in 1974, due in part to the OPEC oil embargo and the accompanying "energy crisis." Chrysler was hit especially hard, suffering a sales drop of thirty-four percent; the company attempted to rectify the situation with the 1975 Cordoba, the shortest Chrysler since World War Two. Billed as "the new small Chrysler," the car remains most memorable for its TV spots, in which actor Ricardo Montalban seductively extolled such extras as "rich, Corinthian leather."

The quintessential 1970s automobile was probably The Pacer, introduced by AMC as "the first wide small car." The car's bubble-like styling made it look like some "car of the future" from a 1950s showroom, but its heavy six-cylinder engine made handling awkward, and caused the car to gobble far more fuel than the average domestic subcompact. For all its hype, sales were disappointing, and the Pacer barely made it to the end of the decade.

Experiencing far more longevity was the "monster truck" craze, inspired by Robert Chandler's **Bigfoot**—a souped-up Ford with four-foot high tires, named after the hairy, ape-like creature currently popping up all over the Pacific Northwest. At county fairs across the country, people flocked to see Chandler demonstrate Bigfoot's prowess, which usually involved rolling over heaps of junked cars.

Evel Genius

Folks also came from all over to see daredevil Robert Craig "Evel" Knievel jump Idaho's Snake River Canyon on September 8. The staunchly right-wing Knievel became one of the most unlikely heroes of the 1970s, idolized both by the denizens of America's myriad trailer parks, and by hyperactive young boys who tried to jump trash cans and other obstacles with their bikes, in emulation of the man who'd allegedly broken every bone in his body two or three times. The latter demographic was undoubtedly a factor in the US government's ban on European mopeds, although officials finally relaxed anti-moped regulations in 1974. As a result, more than two hundred and fifty thousand of the half-bike-half-motorcycles were sold by 1977.

New Handles

Of course, the one drawback to a moped was that there was no room on it for your Citizen's Band radio. CB radio, primarily the domain of truckers who used it as a way to warn each other in code of speed traps and other manifestations of the highway patrol (aka "Smokey the Bear"), suddenly took off in 1974. Two million new CB radio licenses were issued in 1974,

TOP SINGLES

BARBRA STREISAND
"The Way We Were"

TERRY JACKS
"SEASONS IN THE SUN"

RAY STEVENS
"The Streak"

PAUL ANKA
"(You're) Having My Baby"

MFSB
"TSOP (The Sound Of Philadelphia)"

'74 Bigfoot, the world's first monster truck, steps out in style at its press launch.

IN THE NEWS

January – A Gallup poll shows that 79 percent of American voters are in favor of impeaching President Nixon.

February 5 – Patricia Hearst, daughter of publisher Randolph Hearst, is kidnapped in Berkeley, California by members of the Symbionese Liberation Army. The radicals demand ransom of $70 in food for every poor person in California; the Hearst family begins $2,000,000 food giveaway on February 22.

February 6 – An House Judiciary Committee impeachment inquiry against Nixon is approved by the House of Representatives.

March 18 – Arabs lift oil embargo against US following Henry Kissinger's diplomatic missions to Egypt and Israel.

April 3 – Patricia Hearst announces that she has changed her name to Tania and is joining the Symbionese Liberation Army of her own free will. On April 15, a bank camera takes a picture of her participating in a bank robbery.

April 8 – Nixon signs bill to raise the minimum wage to $2.30 an hour.

May 17 – Police open fire on Symbionese Liberation Army headquarters in LA, leaving six of eight known members dead. Patty Hearst was not in the building at the time.

July 24 – The Supreme Court orders the White House to honor Leon Jaworski's subpoena of tapes and documents, ruling that executive privilege does not apply to Watergate-related evidence.

August 5 – Nixon releases tapes and transcripts which reveal his approval the Watergate cover-up.

'74 KO'd in Kinshasa—Foreman takes a punishing right from Ali.

twice the number of licenses issued between 1958 and 1973. Dictionaries of CB lingo became hot sellers, and expressions like "Ten-four, good buddy" (ie, "Yes, sir") quickly entered the mainstream lexicon.

Rumble In The Jungle

In baseball, Henry "Hank" Aaron entered the record books by breaking Babe Ruth's career record of 714 home runs. Although the media was generally more supportive of Aaron than they had been of Roger Maris, many fans behaved much worse, sending him piles of racist hate mail. Despite these distractions, Aaron remained true to his mission, hitting home run number 715 on April 8th, and finishing the season with 733.

In a comeback that had taken the better part of a decade, Muhammad Ali regained the World Heavyweight title, defeating George Foreman in a brutal match held in Kinshasa, Zaire.

Music News

Hand-to-hand combat was all over the radio, in the form of Carl Douglas' "Kung Fu Fighting." Inspired by the current mania for all things martial-arts-related (even the GI Joe action figure now featured "Kung Fu Grip"), the deliciously absurd song topped the December charts—helped, no doubt, by promotional TV appearances in which Douglas traded Kung Fu moves with *ghi*-attired dancers.

There were thirty-five different Number One pop singles in 1974, the most ever for a single year, and the diversity of AM radio playlists now bordered on the schizophrenic. Singles buyers were snapping up everything, including novelty hits, teeny-bop pop (Bo Donaldson and The Heywoods' "Billy, Don't Be A Hero," Andy Kim's "Rock Me Gently"), disco soul (The Hues Corporation's "Rock the Boat," George McRae's "Rock Your Baby"), polished hard rock (Bachman-Turner Overdrive's "You Ain't Seen Nothin' Yet," Grand Funk's cover of "The Loco-Motion"), and folky ballads by Gordon Lightfoot ("Sundown"), Harry Chapin ("Cat's In The Cradle"), and John Denver ("Sunshine On My Shoulders," "Annie's Song").

Stevie Wonder topped the charts with "You Haven't Done Nothin'," a vicious attack on President Nixon, but **Barry White** was all about love (pronounced "*Luuuuuvv*"), scoring with "Can't Get Enough of Your Love, Babe" and "You're The First, The Last, My Everything," as well as writing, producing, and conducting "Love's Theme" for The Love Unlimited Orchestra.

TOP ALBUMS

Elton John	***Greatest Hits***
Jim Croce	***You Don't Mess Around With Jim***
Marvin Hamlisch	***The Sting*** **soundtrack**
Paul McCartney and Wings	***Band On The Run***
Elton John	***Caribou***

Cool And Collected

Intent on getting some value for their money, Americans took home a number of "Best of" albums. John Denver's *Greatest Hits* and Crosby, Stills, Nash and Young's *So Far* were huge sellers, as was *Photographs and Memories*, a collection of hits by Chicago singer-songwriter Jim Croce ("Bad Bad Leroy Brown"), who had died the previous year in a plane crash. *Endless Summer*, a compilation of Beach Boys hits from the early 1960s, totally turned the group's career around; as a new generation of kids discovered the joys of "Fun, Fun, Fun" and "California Girls," The Beach Boys were once again in high demand as a concert draw.

TV News

The theatrical success of last year's *American Graffiti* paved the way for *Happy Days*, a popular comedy nostalgically set in a blurry late-fifties/early sixties time period. The show featured *American Graffiti*'s Ron Howard (who, a decade earlier, had played Opie on *The Andy Griffith Show*), and made a surprise star out of Henry Winkler, who played the leather-jacketed, preternaturally cool Arthur "**The Fonz**" Fonzarelli. Recurring Fonz expressions like "Sit on it!" and "Aaaaay!" (accompanied by an affirmative thumbs-up gesture) were some of the most oft-repeated phrases of 1974-75, rivalled only by "Dy-No-Mite!," which was shouted *ad nauseam* by Jimmy ("JJ") Walker on *Good Times*.

Other popular new comedies included *Chico and the Man* (starring comedian Freddie Prinze) and *Rhoda*, a *Mary Tyler Moore* spin-off starring Valerie Harper.

The Rockford Files and ***Police Woman*** were two of the year's most popular crime shows; the former featured James Garner as a down-on-his-luck private eye, while the latter starred Angie

'74 Jack Nicholson in *Chinatown*

Dickinson as Sgt Pepper Anderson, an undercover LAPD officer who always seemed to have to impersonate a prostitute when solving a case. Other new shows, *Little House on the Prairie* (based on Laura Ingalls Wilder's books about life as a pioneer family in the 1870s) and ***The Six Million Dollar Man*** (starring Lee Majors as "Steve Austin, a man barely alive..."), were big favorites with the kids.

Movie Audiences Quake In Their Seats

While 1974 produced some truly great films (Francis Ford Coppola's *The Godfather Part II*, Roman Polanski's *Chinatown*), it also gave us some really memorable trash. *Airport 1975* continued in the air-disaster vein of the original (but was set this time on—ooh!—a 747), while *The Towering Inferno* menaced Steve McQueen and an all-star cast of thousands with a flaming skyscraper. *Earthquake*, an almost unwatchably bad disaster film starring the ubiquitous Charlton Heston, was slightly redeemed by its use of "**Sensurround**," which added rumbling realism to the quake sequences; doctors claimed this new effect damaged your eardrums, but it sure was fun. And who could ever forget Gunnar Hansen wearing a mask of human skin and brandishing Black and Decker's finest hardware in ***The Texas Chainsaw Massacre***? Tobe Hooper's bloody (and extremely frightening) film, loosely based on the ghoulish career Wisconsin farmer Ed Gein, set a new standard for "splatter flicks" and proved enduringly popular with college film clubs.

Mel Brooks' *Young Frankenstein* just slips into the list of great 1974 films. All of his later efforts were pretty terrible; if we're gonna give the man his due, this is probably the best place to do it (though let's not forget 1968's *The Producers*).

'74 *Happy Days'* Howard and Winkler, and *(right)* *The Texas Chainsaw Massacre*.

IN THE NEWS

August 8 – Nixon makes a televised resignation speech; as 100,000,000 people watch on three networks, Nixon admits to having made some wrong decisions, but insists that the real reason he's leaving is because Congress no longer supports him.

August 9 – Nixon resigns. Gerald R Ford sworn in as president.

September 8 – Nixon pardoned by President Ford for any crimes he may have committed or participated in while in office. Ford claims that his actions are motivated by a desire to end the national divisions caused by the Watergate scandal, but the move will effectively doom his re-election campaign in 1976.

September 16 – Ford offers limited amnesty to Vietnam War draft resisters and deserters, on the condition that they swear allegiance to the US and perform up to two years of public service.

December 19 – Nelson A Rockefeller, former Governor of New York, is sworn in as vice-president.

December 21 – *The New York Times* reports that the CIA, during the Nixon administration, had maintained files on some 10,000 US citizens, as well as engaged in illegal domestic operations against opponents of the Vietnam War.

nineteen 75

The Vietnam War ended in 1975,

but nobody in the States seemed to feel much like celebrating. Among most Americans, the pervasive attitude towards the war's ignominious conclusion seemed to be a mixture of relief and embarrassment; unsurprisingly, **there was a conspicuous absence of ticker-tape parades for returning vets.** With food prices at an all-time high, electricity rates up thirty percent from 1974, and unemployment hitting levels not seen since 1941, Americans were more concerned about the prospect of another depression than with healing the scars left by the war.

TOP TELEVISION SHOWS

All in the Family
Sanford and Son
Maude
Rhoda
*M*A*S*H**

ACADEMY AWARDS

Best Picture
One Flew over the Cuckoo's Nest
directed by Milos Forman

Best Actor
Jack Nicholson
One Flew over the Cuckoo's Nest

Best Actress
Louise Fletcher
One Flew over the Cuckoo's Nest

Indeed, there were plenty of new wounds being wrought by forced busing, the government's attempt to desegregate public schools by sending white kids to schools in black neighborhoods, and vice-versa.

First-Family Misfortunes

Gerald Ford's first full year in office was as difficult for him as it was for the rest of the country. His wife Betty caused a stir when, during a televised interview, she lauded the US Supreme Court's controversial 1973 *Roe v Wade* ruling legalizing abortion as a "great, great decision." Shortly thereafter, his son Jack, twenty-three, publicly admitted using marijuana.

'75 As the US pulls out of Vietnam, the Saigon embassy is evacuated.

In September, the president nearly fell victim to not one but *two* assassination attempts—first in Sacramento, California by Manson

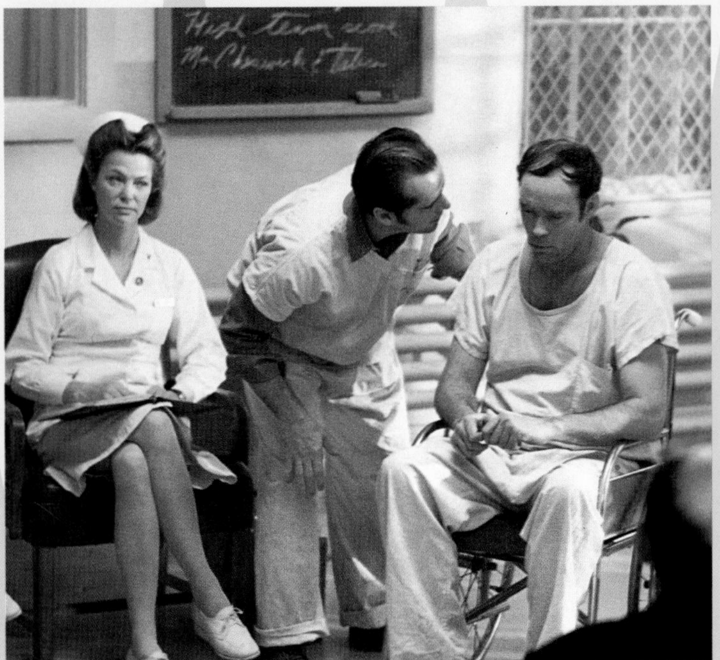

'75 **Monster hits:** ***One Flew over the Cuckoo's Nest*** **and** ***(below) Jaws*****.**

Pepper, *Three Days of the Condor*) and Barbra Streisand (*Funny Lady*) were the year's biggest stars, or rather, the year's biggest *human* stars—"Bruce," the twenty-foot mechanical Great White shark who handily upstaged ***Jaws*** co-stars Roy Scheider, Robert Shaw and Richard Dreyfuss, was easily the year's top box-office attraction. In the wake of the film's runaway success, sharkmania gripped the nation; a puzzle book called *Shark Mazes* was a big seller among schoolkids, shark's-tooth pendants hung from men's necks, and "Mr Jaws," Dickie Goodman's novelty "answer" record, even made it into the Top Five.

follower Lynette A "Squeaky" Fromme, and two weeks later in San Francisco by estranged FBI informant Sara Jane Moore.

Movie News

If the president was getting off to a rather shaky start, Hollywood was running at full steam, raking in a record two billion dollars in profits. Milos Forman's ***One Flew over the Cuckoo's Nest*** (starring Jack Nicholson as the likeable trouble-maker who stirs things up in an insane asylum, and Louise Fletcher as the hard-as-nails Nurse Ratchet) and Robert Altman's *Nashville* garnered heaps of critical plaudits, but it was ultra-violent pictures like *Rollerball* and *Death Race 2000* that really had 'em lining up at the box office.

Warren Beatty slept his way through Beverly Hills in *Shampoo*, and Al Pacino tried to rob a bank to pay for his lover's sex-change operation in *Dog Day Afternoon*. Robert Redford (*The Great Waldo*

IN THE NEWS

February 21 – For their roles in the Watergate cover-up, HR Haldeman, John D Ehrlichman, and John Mitchell are each sentenced to 30 months in prison.

April 30 – The Vietnam War ends, as the last remaining US citizens are air-lifted out of Saigon. Cambodia and South Vietnam fall to Communist forces.

May 12 – The US merchant ship *Mayaguez* is seized in Cambodian waters, and the crew are charged with espionage. On May 14, the 39 crew members are freed by a US military raid which leaves fifteen US soldiers dead and 50 wounded.

July 15 – The US and USSR's joint *Apollo-Soyuz* space mission begins. The Russian and American spacecrafts dock with each other on July 17; the crews perform a number of scientific experiments together during the 44-hour linkup.

July 30 – Former Teamsters Union President Jimmy Hoffa disappears after making a phone call from the Manchus Red Fox Restaurant in suburban Detroit. Though he is presumed murdered by underworld figures, Hoffa's fate has never been officially solved.

Good, Clean Fun?

Perhaps most damaging of all the new president's troubles were Chevy Chase's Ford impersonations on NBC's new *Saturday Night Live*, which mercilessly lampooned his lumbering, slow-on-the-draw demeanor and his propensity for accidental pratfalls. President Ford may not have been a fan of *Saturday Night Live*, but the late-night comedy program was

'75 Love keeps The Captain and Tennille together.

unquestionably one of the year's bright spots. Most of the show's cast (which included Chase, Dan Aykroyd, John Belushi, Jane Curtin, Garrett Morris, Laraine Newman, and Gilda Radner) and writers had been previously involved with various *National Lampoon* projects, a connection evidenced by the show's irreverent (and usually somewhat tasteless) brand of humor, which suited perfectly the cynical tenor of the times.

Across the dial, ABC weighed in with the similarly titled—and far less successful—*Saturday Night Live with Howard Cosell*. Though the verbose Cosell seemed far more comfortable in his regular gig as an ABC sportscaster than as the host of a variety show, the program did feature regular appearances by talented comedian Bill Murray, who coincidentally would go on to replace Chevy Chase as a member of NBC's *SNL* cast in the fall of 1976.

Thanks to the National Association of Broadcasters' new emphasis on "family viewing time," network affiliated stations were encouraged to set aside two hours in the early evening as a sex- and violence-free zone; the stations generally made the best of the situation by programming syndicated game shows and sitcoms. *Welcome Back, Kotter,* starring Gabe Kaplan as a high-school teacher saddled with a group of under-achieving students known as "The Sweathogs," was one of the year's most popular new sitcoms; **John Travolta** got his first big break in show business as Vinnie Barbarino, an exceptionally dim-witted member of the class.

Up-Beat Cops

All in the Family and *The Mary Tyler Moore Show* continued to produce popular new spin-offs (*The Jeffersons* and *Phyllis*, respectively). *Barney Miller* was one of the few violence-free cop shows on the air, while newcomers *SWAT*, *Baretta,* and *Starsky and Hutch* had gunplay and grittiness to spare. The latter two shows at least offered occasional comic relief; *Baretta*'s Robert Blake spent a portion of each episode communing with his pet cockatoo, Fred, while ***Starsky and Hutch***'s Antonio Fargas played Huggy Bear, the jive-talking informer to end all jive-talking informers.

West Meets East

The Night Stalker and *Kung Fu*, two of the decade's most intriguing shows, were canceled by ABC halfway through the year. One of the few horror shows to actually boast some good scares, *The Night Stalker* starred Darren McGavin as Carl Kolchak, a rumpled Chicago reporter constantly doing battle with the forces of evil. Forever insisting that "I come in peace," ***Kung Fu***'s Kwai Chang Caine (David Carradine) had ample opportunity to showcase his slow-motion martial arts skills, usually against cowboys who reacted to his exotic presence with greetings of, "I'm gon' *kill* you, Chinaman!" The show was also famous for its atmospheric flashback sequences, during which the young "Grasshopper" Caine pondered pearls of inscrutable wisdom at the knee of blind Master Po.

Winning Game Plans

Possessing a similar Zen-like intensity was Pong, the video table tennis game that hooked up to your television set. Invented by Atari founder Nolan Bushnell, the home version of Pong sold one hundred and fifty thousand units in its first year on the market, kick-starting the whole home videogame craze in the process. Meanwhile, over at the local arcade, Bally's new Wizard (a pinball game based on Ken Russell's film of The Who's *Tommy*) was working overtime coaxing hard-earned quarters from the pockets of pinball fanatics.

Car Industry Cutbacks

"It's about time for a new kind of American car," sang the ads for Chevrolet's new Chevette, an economical (if plain-looking) sub-compact that could get up to thirty-five miles per gallon on the highway. In truth, it was time for any kind of American car that could bring consumers into the showrooms. On February 3, auto industry layoffs cut Detroit's automotive workforce by over thirty-three percent, with poor sales taking most of the blame.

Still, some makes and models were selling well. Ford's new Granada, a slightly smaller and more fuel-conscious version of the Ford Maverick, quickly became the company's top-

TOP SINGLES

The Captain and Tennille
"Love Will Keep Us Together"

Silver Convention
"Fly, Robin, Fly"

Elton John
"Island Girl"

Neil Sedaka
"Bad Blood"

Tony Orlando and Dawn
"He Don't Love You (Like I Love You)"

TOP ALBUMS

ELTON JOHN
Captain Fantastic And the Brown Dirt Cowboy

LED ZEPPELIN
Physical Graffiti

THE EAGLES
One Of These Nights

CHICAGO
Chicago IX: Chicago's Greatest Hits

JEFFERSON STARSHIP
Red Octopus

selling car, while Cadillac's new Seville, an "intermediate" luxury vehicle *à la* Mercedes-Benz, racked up sales of forty-three thousand.

Van-Tastic!

If the fifties and early sixties produced a rash of car-oriented songs, it's only appropriate that it took one of 1975's biggest singles to finally give vans their due. Whether you were traveling in the "Mystery Machine" with *Scooby-Doo* and the gang, or just pulling bongs in the back of a Dodge Econoline airbrushed with a scene out of Norse mythology, the customized van was like a clubhouse on wheels for the groovy youngsters of the early and mid-seventies. A Top Five hit, Sammy Johns' "Chevy Van" perfectly encapsulated the van fantasy: Man in van picks up nubile hitchhiker; man has sex with hitchhiker in back of van (whose interior is doubtless covered in thick shag carpeting); man deposits hitchhiker in out-of-the-way town and drives on. This archetypal scenario was later the basis for *The Van*, a 1976 film starring a pre-*Taxi* Danny DeVito.

Meet The New Boss...

Similarly vehicular-minded (although a good deal more romantic), Bruce Springsteen's new *Born To Run* LP sold like hot cakes and landed the scraggly New Jersey singer on the covers of *Time* and *Newsweek* in the same week. Springsteen's three-hour concerts were the stuff of legend, causing many rock critics to swoon like schoolgirls. Also legendary were the incendiary live performances of **Kiss**, the fire-breathing, blood-spitting, makeup-wearing rock band that all the critics seemed to hate. Although it received almost no support from radio or the media, word of mouth and nonstop touring helped their live *Kiss Alive* album slither into the Top Ten.

'75 Barry Manilow.

The Magic of Manilow

Flamboyant soft-rocker Barry Manilow had a fabulous year, scoring huge hits with "Mandy," "Could it Be Magic," "It's a Miracle," and "I Write The Songs." A former jingle writer and erstwhile Bette Midler accompanist, Manilow became an instant heart-throb of America's housewife set.

Blown Away

All-in-one stereos (which, like Zenith's "The Wedge," usually included AM/FM receiver, an eight-track tape recorder and a turntable) were especially popular among seventies music buyers. Also popular were portable eight-track players, the most memorable being the Panasonic Dynamite 8, which came in a variety of bright colors and looked like a detonator; just pop in your favorite rock eight-track, and push down on the handle for an explosion of sound.

Emotional Appeal

Of course, as anyone in 1975 could've told you, nothing rocked like the Pet Rock. The brainchild of California businessman Gary Dahl, the Pet Rock was the year's hottest-selling novelty gift. Costing a mere four dollars, the rocks came in miniature pet carrying-cases filed with straw, accompanied by an owner's manual that told you how to teach your pet to roll over, play dead, and generally be on its best behavior.

Almost as popular (and just as memorable) were **Mood Rings**, whose heat-sensitive liquid crystal stones supposedly changed color according to your mood. Black meant you were anxious or excitable, amber meant nervous or tense, green meant sensitive, red meant passionate, blue meant happy, and it only cost $19.95 to figure out what you were feeling.

IN THE NEWS

September 18 – Patrica Hearst captured by the FBI in San Francisco. She is indicted October 2 on charges of assault, robbery and kidnapping.

November 10 – The New Jersey Superior Court denies the parents of Karen Anne Quinlan the right to turn off their comatose daughter's life-support system. Although Karen Anne's condition is irreversible, the court rules that she is not legally or medically dead. The New Jersey Supreme Court reverses the decision in March 1976.

November 26 – President Ford announces his support for a short-term federal loan of $2.3 billion to New York City, in order to help America's largest city avoid bankruptcy.

Cosmic Cash for Football Star

In the world of sports, Brazilian soccer star **Pelé** (born Edson Arantes do Nascimento) came out of retirement to play for the New York Cosmos of the North American Soccer League, thanks to a three-year, seven-million-dollar contract that made him the world's highest-paid team athlete. Cosmos executives hoped that his presence would help boost the sport's popularity in America.

nineteen 76

America celebrated its two-hundredth birthday in 1976, and the entire country seemed to be swathed in stars and stripes. Eveywhere you looked, people were painting fire hydrants in shades of red, white, and blue, donning tri-colored clown wigs, and plunking down newly minted Bicentennial twenty-five-cent and dollar coins for clothes, dishes, coffee mugs and anything else with a flag pattern on it.

TOP TELEVISION SHOWS

- *Happy Days*
- *Laverne and Shirley*
- *The Six Million Dollar Man*
- *M*A*S*H*
- *The Bionic Woman*

The Bicentennial celebrations culminated on July 4 with the nationwide ringing of bells, the convergence of fifty warships and sixteen tall ships from around the world in New York harbor, and the largest display of fireworks anyone had ever seen. In retrospect, the timing couldn't have been better. For all its gaudiness and self-congratulation, the Bicentennial did a lot to bring the country back together after the divisive traumas of the Vietnam era. Not coincidentally, most Bicentennial celebrations seemed to downplay America's military might, highlighting instead the country's domestic accomplishments and the resilience of its people.

America Reborn With Carter

It's hard to imagine another year in the late twentieth century in which Jimmy Carter could have been elected president. A peanut farmer and former one-term Governor of Georgia, Carter was the perfect candidate for a country grown increasingly cynical about lawyers and career politicians. Both Miss Lillian, Carter's mother, and Billy, his down-home younger brother, became national celebrities thanks to their outspoken ways (Jimmy himself proved almost too outspoken, nearly capsizing his campaign by admitting to *Playboy* that he had "committed adultery in my heart many times"), and Carter generally exuded a warmth and sincerity that contrasted strongly with Gerald Ford's almost Frankensteinian stiffness. Of course, Ford's inability to stem the rising inflation and unempoyment rates was certainly a decisive factor in the election, but when Carter pledged "**I will never lie to you**," many Americans took him at his word. It's interesting to note that Carter was the first (and, to date, the only) "born again" Christian to be elected to the White House. Although his own politics were moderately liberal, Carter's election presaged the rise in profile and power of the religious right during the next decade.

'76 Rocky *(left)* suffers but Laverne and Shirley *(above)* bloom.

'76 Keitel and De Niro in *Taxi Driver*, and Sissy Spacek *(right)* in *Carrie*.

Movie News

Despite its humiliation in Vietnam, America maintained its status as the wealthiest and most powerful nation in the world, yet most Americans still instinctively identified with rebels and underdogs. *Rocky*, starring **Sylvester Stallone** as a boxer who gets a "million to one" shot at the world heavyweight boxing title, was the ultimate underdog tale; the previously unknown Stallone had risked his entire savings to bring his script to the screen, a fact with gave the already uplifting film an added bit of resonance. The film was a runaway smash, and Stallone became a matinee idol literally overnight.

Less uplifting, but equally resonant, was Sidney Lumet's ***Network***, an amazingly prescient satire of network television; Peter Finch's crazed admission that "I'm mad as hell, and I'm not gonna take it anymore!" became one of the seventies' most familiar battle cries, along with Robert De Niro's "You lookin' at me?" from Martin Scorsese's unbelievably seamy ***Taxi Driver***.

Robert Redford (who starred with Dustin Hoffman as Bob Woodward and Carl Bernstein in *All The President's Men*) and thirteen-year-old Tatum O'Neal (*The Bad News Bears, Nickelodeon*) were the year's biggest male and female draws. John Wayne made his last film appearance as a dying gunfighter in *The Shootist*, while Barbra Streisand and Kris Kristofferson tried unsuccessfully to breathe new life into *A Star is Born*. Another remake, Dino DeLaurentis' *King Kong* sent the titular ape to the top of New York's World Trade Center, but had little other than ace special effects to recommend it. Much better were horror films ***Carrie*** and ***The Omen***; the former starred Sissy Spacek as a telekinetic teenager who lays waste to her teasing classmates, while the latter featured Gregory Peck and Lee Remick as a couple who come to the unsettling realization that their son is the anti-Christ.

ACADEMY AWARDS

Best Film
Rocky
directed by John G Avildsen

Best Actor
Peter Finch
Network

Best Actress
Faye Dunaway
Network

Stay Hungry gave Austrian bodybuilder Arnold Schwarzenegger his first major film role, while *Logan's Run*, a futuristic look at a world of compulsory pleasure, got much of its box-office juice from a supporting appearance by one of television's hottest new stars: Farrah Fawcett-Majors.

Superwomen Take Over TV

Debuting in the fall of 1976, *Charlie's Angels* immediately took the television world by storm. As three gorgeous detectives capable of tackling any case, Kate Jackson, Jaclyn Smith and **Farrah Fawcett-Majors** became the idols of millions of young girls, and the lust objects of millions of American males; all feathered blonde hair and shiny teeth, Farrah (who was married at the time to *Six Million Dollar Man* Lee Majors) was the most popular pin-up to come along in years. Other female superheroes popping up on television in 1976 included *The Bionic Woman*, a *Six Million Dollar Man* spin-off starring Lindsay Wagner, and ***Wonder Woman***, starring Lynda Carter as the Nazi-fighting Amazon princess, while Electra-Woman (Deidre Hall) and Dynagirl (Judy Strangis) were regulars on Saturday morning's *Krofft Supershow*. Living slightly more mundane existences were *Alice*, a widowed mother and waitress played by Linda Lavin, and Louise Lasser's titular Ohio housewife in the soap-opera parody ***Mary Hartman, Mary Hartman***.

Of the year's new sitcoms, *Laverne and Shirley* (a *Happy Days* spin-off starring Penny Marshall and Cindy Williams) and *What's Happening!!* (an updated version of the 1975 film *Cooley High*, itself something of a black *American Graffiti*) were easily the most popular. Also doing quite well were musical variety shows starring The Captain and Tennille ("Love Will Keep Us Together"), Donny and Marie Osmond, and Jim Henson's Muppets.

For *real* bottom-of-the-barrel entertainment, you couldn't beat ***The Gong Show***, a talent show wherein the celebrity judges regularly negated contestants by rapping a large gong. Host/co-producer Chuck Barris was a true renaissance man; not only was he responsible for those twin pillars of popular culture, *The Dating Game* and *The Newlywed Game*, but he also wrote "Palisades Park" for Freddy Cannon in 1962.

John Travolta further cemented his teen-heartthrob status as the lead in *The Boy in the Plastic Bubble*, an ABC Friday Night Movie. Travolta also managed to score two Top Forty hits—"Let Her In" and "Whenever I'm Away From You"—though he would have to wait another year for his disco apotheosis.

'76 Arnie—hungry for stardom.

Music News

In 1976, there were an estimated ten thousand discos open in the United States, as opposed to only fifteen hundred in 1974. The hustle, a combination of mambo and jitterbug steps, was the favored dance of the day, although the bump was almost as popular. Cheaper than going to a rock concert and less hassle than a singles

IN THE NEWS

February 18 – President Ford issues an executive order curtailing domestic surveillance of US citizens by the FBI and CIA.

May 28 – The US and USSR sign a nuclear test pact limiting underground tests to a maximum of 150 kilotons; the pact also allows the US to inspect Soviet test sites.

July 14 – Former Georgia governor James Earl "Jimmy" Carter, Jr is nominated for president at the Democratic convention. Senator Walter Mondale is nominated for vice-president the next day.

July 20 – *Viking 1*, launched eleven months earlier, lands on Mars. *Viking 2* lands on Mars on September 3. Both spacecraft collect data showing the planet to be barren, rocky—and generally devoid of Martians.

August 19 – The Republican National Convention narrowly nominates Gerald Ford for re-election over Ronald Reagan. Senator Robert Dole is nominated for the vice-presidency.

September 1 – Ohio Representative Wayne Hays resigns from the US House of Representatives in the wake of a sex scandal involving him and former secretary Elizabeth Ray.

September 17 – In light of recent revelations of malfeasance and abuse of power by the country's intelligence agencies, a special committee to review the assassinations of John F Kennedy and Martin Luther King, Jr is created by the House of Representatives.

September 24 – Patricia Hearst sentenced to seven years in jail for her participation in a 1974 bank robbery.

TOP ALBUMS

Stevie Wonder
Songs In The Key of Life

Peter Frampton
Frampton Comes Alive!

Wings
Wings At The Speed Of Sound

Bob Dylan
Desire

The Eagles
Greatest Hits, 1971–1975

bar, the disco was a combination of both, one which also allowed gays, straights, blacks, and whites to party together as one underneath the mirror ball.

Arena Yields To The Ramones

There was still an audience for rock records, as evidenced by the phenomenal success of Boston's first album, The Steve Miller Band's *Fly Like An Eagle*, Heart's *Dreamboat Annie*, and Kiss's *Destroyer*. New York's Ramones didn't exactly storm the Top Forty with their self-titled debut, but their loud-and-fast aesthetic made a positive impression on many music fans and critics sick of the bloated excesses of arena rock. The P-Funk Earth Tour, led by funk pied piper George Clinton, landed the Parliament-Funkadelic mothership in sold-out arenas across the country, but most older black acts had a tough time in the disco era. Johnnie Taylor, who had a number five hit in 1968 with "Who's Making Love," was one of the few to successfully

'76 The Ramones

make the adjustment, topping the charts for four weeks with "**Disco Lady**," a cash-in almost as blatant as CW McCall's "**Convoy**," which capitalized on the Citizen's Band radio craze by using CB lingo to recount a tale of renegade truckers.

Volare Takes Off

Due to declining sales, US auto companies ceased production of convertibles in 1976; Cadillac's El Dorado was the last convertible model released. One of the few bright spots for Detroit was the success of Plymouth's Volare; thanks to a memorable ad campaign featuring crooner Sergio Franchi, the upscale compact sold four hundred thousand units in its first year on the market.

Videogame News

Encouraged by the success of Atari, other companies tried dipping their joysticks into the home videogame market. Coleco introduced Telstar Pong, while the Fairchild Camera and Instrument Company weighed in with the Fairchild Channel F; the first programmable home game console, it came with large cartridges that could be inserted in order to play different games.

Cutting-Edge Style

After winning a gold medal at the Winter Olympics in Innsbruck, Austria, US figure skater Dorothy Hamill quickly became an icon for young girls, who adopted Dorothy's "Wedge" haircut as their own—at least until Farrah showed up. Bruce Jenner also become a national hero for winning the Decathalon at the Summer Olympics in Montreal, but exerted little sartorial influence on the country's youth. Nor did many folks adopt the grown-out Harpo Marx hairdo of Mark "The Bird" Fidrych, the rookie pitcher who won nineteen games for the lowly Detroit Tigers. So named for his resemblance to *Sesame Street*'s Big Bird, "The Bird" was famous for talking to the ball between pitches; the technique's effectiveness only lasted for one season, however, and Fidrych was out of baseball completely after only a couple of years.

Having narrowly defeating Ken Norton in a Heavyweight title bout, **Muhammad Ali** announced his retirement from boxing, a pledge that proved about as realistic as the then-circulating rumor that Bubble Yum bubblegum contained spider eggs. Within a year, Ali would be back in the ring.

IN THE NEWS

September 27 – Carter and Ford face off in a televised debate before an audience of 90 million viewers. Although neither candidate is a clear-cut victor, Carter scores well a week later when Ford blows the second debate by declaring "There is no Soviet domination of Eastern Europe."

September 30 – California passes the first state "right to die" law, which grants adults the right to authorize physicians to turn off their life-support system if death is imminent.

November 2 – James Earl "Jimmy" Carter, Jr elected president by a margin of 1.7 million votes.

November 12 – Normalization talks begin in Paris between the US and Vietnam, although US opposition to Vietnam's application for UN membership is a sore point.

TOP SINGLES

Rod Stewart
"Tonight's The Night (Gonna Be Alright)"

Wings
"Silly Love Songs"

Elton John and Kiki Dee
"Don't Go Breaking My Heart""

Johnnie Taylor
"Disco Lady"

Wild Cherry
"Play That Funky Music"

nineteen 77

1977 was yet **another banner year for the movie industry,** with box-office registers ringing to the tune of $2.3 billion in revenues thanks to the holy trinity of *Star Wars, Close Encounters of the Third Kind,* and *Saturday Night Fever.* **Kids of all ages flocked repeatedly to see Luke Skywalker** (Mark Hamill) and Han Solo (Harrison Ford) take on Darth Vader's Death Star with the help of a couple of robots and a Wookie.

TOP TELEVISION SHOWS

Laverne and Shirley
Happy Days
Charlie's Angels
*M*A*S*H*
Three's Company

ACADEMY AWARDS

Best Picture
Annie Hall
directed by Woody Allen

Best Actor
Richard Dreyfuss
The Goodbye Girl

Best Actress
Diane Keaton
Annie Hall

Star Wars bubblegum cards, toys, watches, masks, towels, T-shirts and records sold in unimaginable numbers, and the phrase "May the Force be with you" became a part of everyday conversation. Unlike *Star Wars*, Steven Spielberg's ***Close Encounters*** was less *Flash Gordon* and more *War of the Worlds*, only with suitably updated special effects and an uplifting ending.

Saturday Night Fever, which came out later in the year, featured John Travolta (in his first leading film role) playing Brooklyn disco king Tony Manero. The film's success pushed the already thriving disco scene to new heights of popularity; male disco denizens everywhere copied Travolta's white-suit-and-dark-shirt look, usually set off with gold chains and Italian snaggle-tooth pendants. Flared slacks and platform shoes also became an integral part of the disco look, along with form-fitting, vividly patterned polyester shirts.

Many women picked up on Diane Keaton's unorthodox ***Annie Hall*** wardrobe; ensembles consisting of

'77 Diane Keaton and Woody Allen in *Annie Hall*, aptly subtitled *A Nervous Romance*.

floppy hats, oversized men's shirts, tise, vests, and baggy chinos were soon spotted on the streets of most major metropolitan areas. Though already highly regarded for a string of hilarious films that included 1969's *Take the Money and Run*, 1971's *Bananas* and 1973's *Sleeper*, Woody Allen had his greatest commercial and critical success to date with *Annie Hall*.

Completely reviled by critics, *Smokey and the Bandit* was a box-office smash. Starring **Burt Reynolds** as a daredevil bootlegger endlessly pursued by small-town sheriff Jackie Gleason, the film proved (as did *Semi-Tough*, his other 1977 project) that audiences would pay to see Reynolds in just about anything. Arnold Schwarzenegger would have to wait until the next decade for similar treatment, although *Pumping Iron*, George Butler's documentary about the Mr Olympia bodybuilding championships, went a long way towards establishing "Ah-nold" as an appealing screen personality.

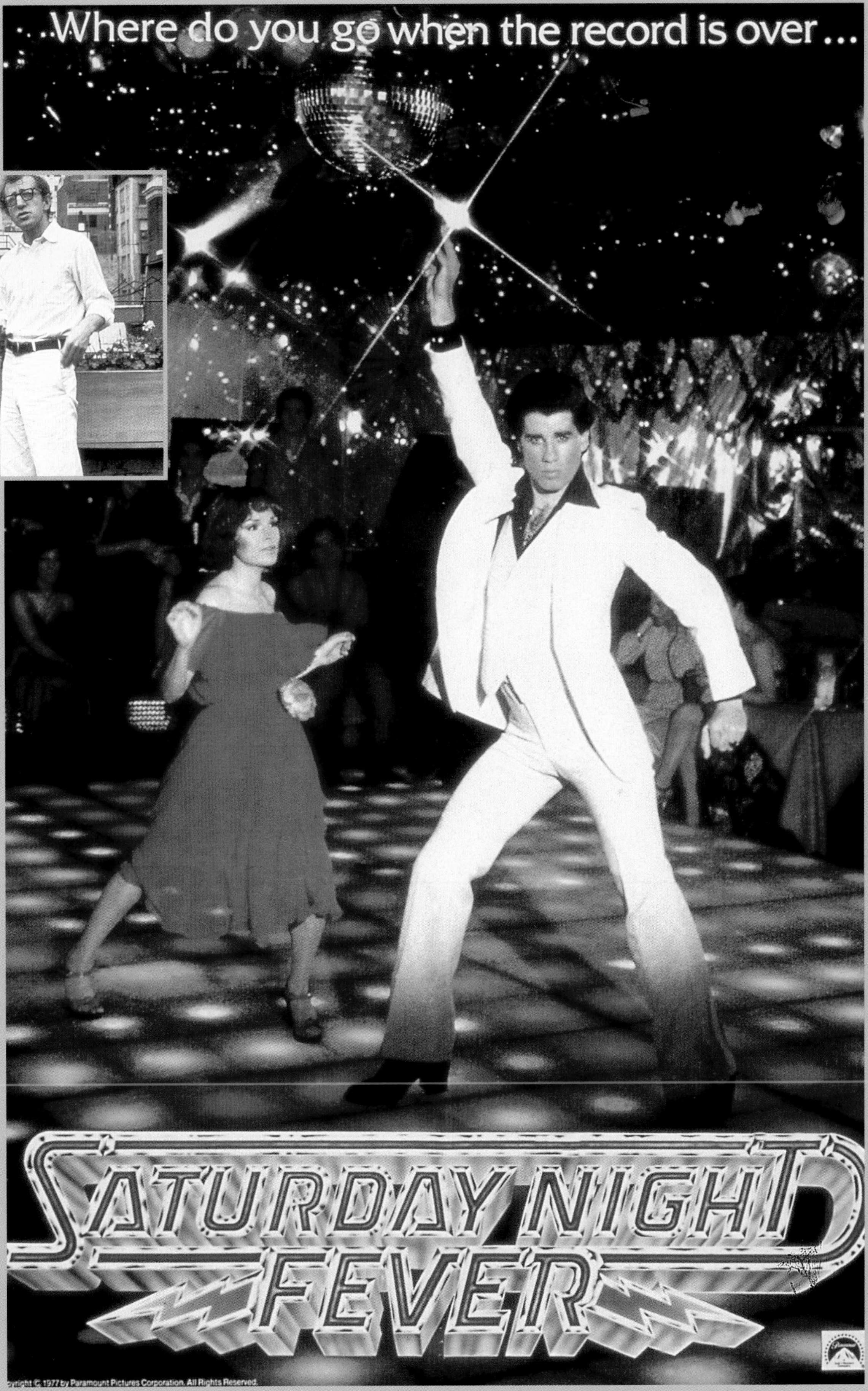

...Where do you go when the record is over...

SATURDAY NIGHT FEVER

TV News

The big news in TV land was Farrah Fawcett-Majors' decision to leave *Charlie's Angels* after only a year, ostensibly to pursue film projects. Her replacement, Cheryl Ladd, became almost as popular a pin-up as Farrah, as did Suzanne Somers, star of the hot new sitcom *Three's Company*. *Chico and the Man*'s Freddie Prinze chose to leave his show in a much more dramatic manner—with a bullet in his head. Overwhelmed by sudden fame and a nagging drug problem, the twenty-two-year-old comic shot himself to death in January.

Other popular new shows included *The Love Boat*, *Lou Grant* (featuring Ed Asner in a serious take on his *Mary Tyler Moore Show* character), and *CHiPs*, an action series starring Erik Estrada and Larry Wilcox as California Highway Patrolmen. ***The Life and Times of Grizzly Adams*** and ***The Man from Atlantis*** were big favorites with younger viewers; the former starred Dan Haggerty as a fugitive from justice (over a crime he didn't commit, of course) who lived in the woods of the Pacific Northwest with a large grizzly bear, while the latter starred Patrick Duffy as a web-footed, acquatic native of a lost continent. Also popular with the kiddies (especially pre-pubescent girls) were *The Hardy Boys*, played by Parker Stevenson and Shaun Cassidy (younger brother of former teen idol David).

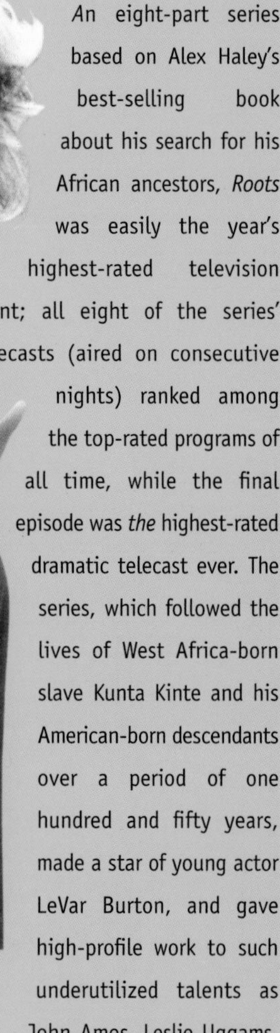

'77 Runaway success—Farrah Fawcett-Majors.

Roots Rated

An eight-part series based on Alex Haley's best-selling book about his search for his African ancestors, *Roots* was easily the year's highest-rated television event; all eight of the series' telecasts (aired on consecutive nights) ranked among the top-rated programs of all time, while the final episode was *the* highest-rated dramatic telecast ever. The series, which followed the lives of West Africa-born slave Kunta Kinte and his American-born descendants over a period of one hundred and fifty years, made a star of young actor LeVar Burton, and gave high-profile work to such underutilized talents as John Amos, Leslie Uggams, and Ben Vereen.

Tut-Mania

Next to *Roots*, King Tut was the biggest American obsession of 1977. For the first time since their excavation in the 1920s, the contents of the ancient Egyptian King Tutankhamen's tomb made the rounds of American museums; the traveling exhibition set off a mania for all things Egyptian, and gave rise to the brief "**pyramid power**" fad, which claimed that you could harness certain spiritual energies through the judicious placement of pyramids around your household.

The King Is Dead

On August 16, while Americans stood in line for hours at a time in order to gawk at the lavish treasures of King Tut's tomb, the King of Rock and Roll died on the throne of his Graceland Mansion bathroom, aged forty-two. Heart failure aggravated by "straining at stool" was ruled as the official cause of death, although Elvis's prodigious pill-gobbling certainly helped to hasten his end—"Dr Nick," aka Dr George Nichopoulos, had prescribed over eleven thousand depressants, stimulants, and painkillers to Elvis during the last fifteen months of his life. Countless tribute records—including Ronnie McDowell's "The King is Gone," Ral Donner's "The Day the Beat Stopped," and JD Sumner's "Elvis Has Left the Building"—were immediately waxed, and rock 'n' roll fans everywhere went into deep mourning.

Perhaps the saddest thing of all about The King's death was that, at the time he checked out, there was precious little evidence of his influence left on the charts. Of all of 1977's chart-toppers, only Shaun Cassidy's watered-down cover of The Crystals' "Da Doo Ron Ron" actually qualified as rock 'n' roll—and just barely, at that. The punk revolution may have been raging in England, but underground American bands like Television, Talking Heads, and The Dead Boys couldn't even get on the radio, much less compete with the likes of Bill Conti's "Gonna Fly Now (Theme from Rocky)," Alan O'Day's "Undercover Angel," or Mary MacGregor's "Torn Between Two Lovers." **David Soul**, who had spent the earlier part of the decade trying to make it as a masked folksinger known as "The Covered Man," cashed in on his popularity as one-half of *Starsky and Hutch*, and scored a Number One hit with "Don't Give Up On Us." Debby Boone, daughter of whitebread pop scourge Pat, had the biggest hit of the decade with "You Light Up My Life."

As the continued success of Aerosmith, Ted Nugent, and Kiss proved, there was still an audience for loud guitars and bad attitudes, although it seemed to be dwindling under the onslaught of disco and soft

TOP SINGLES

Debby Boone
"You Light Up My Life"

The Emotions
"Best of My Love"

Andy Gibb
"I Just Want To Be Your Everything"

Stevie Wonder
"Sir Duke"

Barbra Streisand
"Love Theme From *A Star Is Born* (Evergreen)"

'77 The King nears the end of his reign.

rock. **Lynyrd Skynyrd**, a hard-drinkin' band that virtually defined the whole "Southern Rock" movement with songs like "Sweet Home Alabama" and "Free Bird," called it a day after October 20, when the crash of their ancient touring plane killed three members, including leader Ronnie Van Zant.

Throwbacks Battle Industrial Blues

In Detroit, the $337 million Renaissance Center complex, which included a seventy-three-story hotel and four thirty-nine-story office blocks, opened its doors. The city hoped that the complex would spur an economic revitalization of the riot-torn downtown area, but nothing of the sort occured. Nor did the city's auto makers have much luck stemming the tide of Japanese and European imports with new subcompacts like Dodge's Omni and Ford's Fiesta. In many ways, the most interesting new models were throwbacks to an earlier era. Chevrolet's 1978 Silver Anniversary Corvette came with a Stingray-like fastback, while Ford's Mustang King Cobra was a throwback to the muscle-car days, sporting tape stripes, a cool snake decal and a 122-horsepower engine. Lincoln's limited-edition Continental Mark V Diamond Jubilee coupe was typically excessive, coming with a gold grille, special midnight-blue metallic paint, and a leather-bound owner's manual and tool kit.

Cheering News

To the surprise of few, Muhammad Ali came out of retirement in 1977, and defeated Ernie Shavers. Baseball attendance was up twenty-four percent from the previous year, but even that sport's popularity was no match for that of football's Dallas Cowboy Cheerleaders. Practically more famous than the Dallas Cowboys themselves, the scantily clad pom-pom girls even served as the basis for a TV movie starring Jane Seymour.

Apple Blossoms

The Atari Video Computer System (later renamed Atari 2600), which included such games as Tank, Pong, Centipede, Galaxian, Breakout and Pole Position, totally dominated the home videogame market upon its release in 1977. Atari also opened the first Chuck E Cheese restaurant, a nightmarish "fun-for-the-whole family" eatery featuring robotic animals and electronic games. In other technological news, twenty-six-year-old Steve Wozniak and twenty-one-year-old Steve Jobs marketed their new invention, the Apple II **personal computer**.

Bottoms Up, Y'All!

Beer-can collecting was a popular hobby in the late 1970s, and few new brands were more sought after than Billy Beer, a heady concoction brewed to the exact specifications of President Carter's beer-swilling brother.

TOP ALBUMS

Fleetwood Mac
Rumours

The Eagles
Hotel California

Barbra Streisand
***A Star Is Born* soundtrack**

Linda Ronstadt
Simple Dreams

Barry Manilow
Barry Manilow Live

IN THE NEWS

July 1 – A severe West Coast drought necessitates water rationing in California.

July 13–14 – A lightning storm causes a 25-hour power blackout in New York City and New York's Westchester County; extensive looting and arson ensues. 3,776 looters are arrested, 100 policemen injured, and $135 million in damage caused.

July 19 – A flood in Johnstown, Pennsylvania kills 76 and causes $200 million in damage.

August 10 – David Berkowitz is arrested in Yonkers, New York for killing six people and wounding seven more during his thirteen-month "Son of Sam" murder spree. Berkowitz claimed that his neighbor's dog told him to do it.

August 12 – The space shuttle *Enterprise* makes its first free flight, after being lifted to an altitude of 25,000 feet on the back of a Boeing 747.

September 7 – President Carter signs treaties transferring control of the Panama Canal to Panama by the year 2000.

September 21 – Bert Lance, the Carter-appointed Director of the Office of Management and Budget, resigns following congressional criticism of his financial practices during his career as a Georgia banker.

November 18–21 – The first National Women's Conference draws 1,442 delegates to Houston, Texas. The conference calls for the passage of the Equal Rights Amendment and the elimination of institutional discrimination.

nineteen 78

Three years **after the end of the Vietnam War,** Hollywood finally felt comfortable enough to tackle the subject. Although Michael Cimino's *The Deer Hunter* had some **unbelievably gripping Vietnam sequences,** it and Hal Ashby's ***Coming Home*** both dealt primarily with the after-effects of the war on everyday existence in America. Like *The Best Years of Our Lives* thirty-two years earlier, both films **touched a nerve with American audiences,** who made them two of the year's bigger hits.

ACADEMY AWARDS

Best Picture
The Deer Hunter
directed by Michael Cimino

Best Actor
Warren Beatty
Heaven Can Wait

Best Actress
Jane Fonda
Coming Home

TOP TELEVISION SHOWS

Laverne and Shirley
Three's Company
Happy Days
Charlie's Angels
Mork and Mindy

American audiences seemed to have a higher tolerance than usual for serious films, if the success of *An Unmarried Woman*, *Interiors*, and *Midnight Express* was anything to go by. *An Unmarried Woman* featured a memorable performance by Jill Clayburgh as a woman trying to deal with the breakup of her marriage, while *Interiors* was Woody Allen's respectable stab at Ingmar Bergman-style family drama. Of the many who sat through Alan Parker's brutal *Midnight Express*, most would probably think twice before trying to smuggle drugs out of Turkey in the future. The surprise comedy hit of the year was *National Lampoon's Animal House*. Set somewhere in the early 1960s, the film followed the anarchic antics of a fraternity house at fictional Faber College, and provided a perfect showcase for John Belushi's manic brand of physical comedy. As cries of

'78 Frathouse fun for Belushi *(above)* and teen romance for Newton-John and Travolta in *Grease*.

"Toga! Toga! Toga!" rang through the air, college kids everywhere re-enacted the film's toga party sequence, and a whole new generation discovered the unintelligible joys of The Kingsmen's "Louie, Louie."

1978 also saw Christopher Reeve save the world in *Superman*, and offered a surplus of music-related films, both good and truly awful. The better ones included *The Last Waltz*, Martin Scorsese's documentary of The Band's final concert, and Steve Rash's *The Buddy Holly Story*, whose stunning performance by Gary Busey (in the title role) more than made up for the liberties the script took with Holly's life. ***Grease***, a film version of the popular Broadway musical, starred John Travolta and Olivia Newton-John as the two halves of a greaser-debutante romance. Much worse were the vapid disco comedy *Thank God It's Friday*, and *FM*, in which a radio station defies its stiff parent company by spinning the rebellious sounds of Linda Ronstadt and Jimmy Buffett. Lamest of all was *Sergeant Pepper's Lonely Hearts Club Band*, record mogul Robert Stigwood's woefully misguided attempt to make movie stars out of The Bee Gees and Peter Frampton.

Horror films proved immensely successful in 1978, with *Damien—The Omen II*, *Magic* and *Invasion of the Body Snatchers* (a remake of the 1956 "pod people" classic) all doing well in the theaters. George Romero's *Dawn of the Dead* was an update of his earlier *Night of the Living Dead*, given a late-seventies twist; instead of attacking a farmhouse (as they did in the 1968 film), Romero's army of zombies invaded a suburban shopping mall. ***Halloween***, a low-budget film by John Carpenter, kicked off a slasher-flick craze that would make millions over the next decade, and effectively introduced the crazed-killer-in-a-hockey-mask archetype to the horror genre.

TV News

"Boss! Boss! Ze plane! Ze plane!" Uttered by the diminutive Herve Vellechaize, these magic words heralded the beginning of each week's ***Fantasy Island*** episode. Villechaize (who played the white-suited assistant to Ricardo Montalban's omniscient Mr. Roarke) was just part of 1978's odd parade of new TV stars—*The Incredible Hulk* featured hearing-imparied bodybuilder Lou Ferrigno; *Diff'rent Strokes* made a star out of Gary Coleman, whose congenital kidney condition made him look much younger than his real age; *Mork and Mindy* starred comedian **Robin Williams** *(below)* as an alien (from planet Ork) given to exclamations of "Shazbat!" and "Na-Nu, Na-Nu," while *Taxi* introduced the bizarre genius of Andy Kaufman to the world. And speaking of bizarre genius, both adjectives (but mostly just the former) were used to describe *The $1.98 Beauty Contest*, a *Gong Show*-like game show (produced by Chuck Barris, of course) hosted by flamboyant comedian Rip Taylor.

Other new shows included *WKRP in Cincinnati*, a radio station sitcom based loosely on *FM*, and *Battlestar Galactica*, a science fiction series whose three-hour, three-million-dollar premiere was said to be the most expensive premiere telecast to date.

Soap Strikes Oil

Far less costly, but much more popular, was ***Dallas***, the highest-rated nighttime soap opera since

TOP SINGLES

The Bee Gees
"Night Fever"

Andy Gibb
"Shadow Dancing"

Chic
"Le Freak"

The Bee Gees
"Stayin' Alive"

Exile
"Kiss You All Over"

IN THE NEWS

February 8 – Egyptian President Anwar Sadat visits the US, urging the country to exert pressure on Israel to negotiate a Middle East peace settlement.

April 7 – President Carter postpones production of the neutron bomb, pending further research.

May 26 – The first legal casino in the US outside of Nevada opens in Atlantic City, New Jersey.

June 6 – Proposition 13, a controversial California constitutional amendment to cut state property taxes by 57 percent wins over California voters. Amendment reduces the state's revenues from $12 billion to $5 billion.

Peyton Place. Revolving around the various philanderings and business dealings of two Texas oil families, the show boasted an attractive cast (including Victoria Principal, Charlene Tilton, Linda Gray, and Patrick Duffy) and starred Larry Hagman as the fantastically amoral JR Ewing.

Fighting Fit

Inflation continued to rise in 1978, but it didn't seem to affect the sales of jogging suits and other sportswear, which went through the roof as the result of a renewed American interest in physical fitness. Major league baseball's popularity was at an all-time high, with a record forty million fans attending games in 1978. In an attempt to rack up similar attendance numbers, the NFL extended the regular football season from fourteen to sixteen games. In boxing, gap-toothed **Leon Spinks** made headlines on February 15 by winning the World Heavyweight title from Muhammad Ali. Ali defeated Spinks in a September 15 rematch, becoming the first heavyweight boxer to regain the title three different times.

Electro Invasion

Atari continued its domination of the home videogame market with the release of Atari Football. Meanwhile, the Midway company imported Space Invaders from Japan; the game quickly became the hottest arcade attraction in the country. Mattel's hand-held Electronic Quarterback sold parti-cularly well at Christmas time, as did other electronic games like Simon, Merlin, and the 2XL talking robot.

Killer Candy?

Also popular with the kids were Pop Rocks, a candy that fizzed noisily when placed in one's mouth. The big rumor going around school

TOP ALBUMS

THE BEE GEES
Saturday Night Fever
soundtrack

Grease
soundtrack

BILLY JOEL
52nd Street

THE ROLLING STONES
Some Girls

BOSTON
Don't Look Back

playgrounds at the time was that "Mikey," a small child who appeared in commercials for Life Cereal, had died after ingesting a combination of Pop Rocks and Coca-Cola.

Music News

One of the year's big television events, at least as far as **Kiss** fans were concerned, was the broadcast of *Kiss Meets the Phantom of the Park*. Filmed at Southern California's Magic Mountain amusement park, the movie featured Kiss as extra-terrestrial superheroes who defeat a mad scientist and his Kiss look-alike robots.

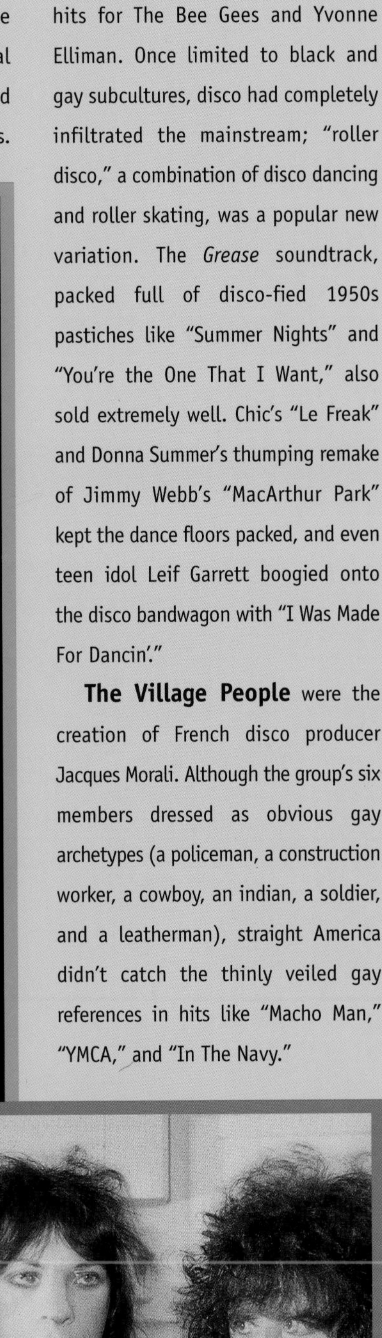

'78 Uninhibited performance artists The Village People, and *(above)* Kiss.

Disco Fever

The *Saturday Night Fever* soundtrack stayed at the top of the album charts for half the year, spawning massive hits for The Bee Gees and Yvonne Elliman. Once limited to black and gay subcultures, disco had completely infiltrated the mainstream; "roller disco," a combination of disco dancing and roller skating, was a popular new variation. The *Grease* soundtrack, packed full of disco-fied 1950s pastiches like "Summer Nights" and "You're the One That I Want," also sold extremely well. Chic's "Le Freak" and Donna Summer's thumping remake of Jimmy Webb's "MacArthur Park" kept the dance floors packed, and even teen idol Leif Garrett boogied onto the disco bandwagon with "I Was Made For Dancin'."

The Village People were the creation of French disco producer Jacques Morali. Although the group's six members dressed as obvious gay archetypes (a policeman, a construction worker, a cowboy, an indian, a soldier, and a leatherman), straight America didn't catch the thinly veiled gay references in hits like "Macho Man," "YMCA," and "In The Navy."

IN THE NEWS

June 28 – In the case of *Bakke v the University of California*, the US Supreme Court rules that the college has to admit white applicant Allan Bakke to its medical school. Bakke claimed his civil rights had been violated by the school's minority-student admission quotas.

August 4 – Having recently discovered that their land was used as a toxic waste dump between 1947 and 1952, the residents of Niagara Falls, New York's Love Canal community begin to evacuate their homes.

September 17 – Anwar Sadat and Israeli Prime Minister Menachem Begin sign an agreement at the White House to conclude a peace treaty between their two nations within three months.

October 6 – Congress extends the deadline for the ratification of the Equal Rights Amendment to June 30, 1982. So far, 35 of the required 38 states have ratified it.

November 18 – 911 people, most of them Americans, commit mass suicide at the People's Temple commune in Guyana. After ordering the murder of California Representative Leo J Ryan, who had come to the commune on a fact-finding mission, Reverend Jim Jones orders the commune's members to drink poisoned Flavoraid.

November 27 – San Francisco Mayor George Moscone and city supervisor Harvey Milk are shot to death at City Hall by disgruntled former supervisor Dan White. White later pleads "Twinkie insanity" (ie, he had been eating too much junk food in the weeks leading up to the attack) and actually receives a reduced sentence.

nineteen 79

1979 was a troubled and troubling year for the United States. Inflation hit 13.3 percent, the highest rate in thirty-three years; thanks to strained relations with the OPEC nations, oil prices were rising as well. Odd-even gas sale days were instituted for motorists in California and many other states; in the East and Midwest, truckers rioted over fuel rationing.

TOP TELEVISION SHOWS

Three's Company
60 Minutes
*M*A*S*H**
Alice
Happy Days

ACADEMY AWARDS

Best Picture
Kramer versus Kramer
directed by Robert Benton

Best Actor
Dustin Hoffman
Kramer versus Kramer

Best Actress
Sally Field
Norma Rae

'79 New Wave band The Knack.

Right-wing Christians responded to what they saw as a direct correlation between the country's troubles and the "decline of American morals" (ie, increased tolerance of drug use, gay rights, and abortion rights) by becoming increasingly politicized. With more than seventy million Americans claiming to be "born again," the Christian Right (or "**Moral Majority**," as they ostentatiously called themselves) were now a political faction to be reckoned with—a fact that would not escape the notice of the Republican Party during the next presidential election.

Fallout Flops

In July, people began to stare nervously at the sky; *Skylab*, the orbiting US space laboratory, was due to re-enter the Earth's atmosphere, but no one knew where the seventy-seven tons of equipment would actually land. On the evening of July 11, revelers across the country painted target symbols on their roofs and held "The Sky is Falling" parties, but eventually went to bed disappointed; the spacecraft, disintegrating upon re-entry, scattered debris over the Indian Ocean and Australia. No injuries were reported, although many Australians were miffed about having their country used as a dumping ground for American space junk.

July also witnessed the introduction of the US Mint's new Susan B. Anthony dollar coin. The first US coin to feature a historical personage of female persuasion, the eleven-sided Anthony dollar was a resounding flop, mostly because of its similarity in size to a twenty-five cent piece—a similarity which caused numerous folks to accidentally spend them in payphones and videogames like Space Invaders and Asteroids.

Discs Slip...

1979's increased oil prices didn't just inconvenience motorists; as petroleum was needed to press records, the shortages hit American record companies squarely in the pocketbook. This development was further compounded by the news that, for the first time in twenty-five years, record sales were slipping. Many industry analysts blamed disco for this turn of events, arguing that most disco fans bought singles, not albums.

While this was a huge over-simplification, disco was indeed an easy scapegoat; with disco music having thoroughly saturated nearly every aspect of the market (*Mickey Mouse Disco*, featuring Donald Duck quacking his way through "Macho Duck," was a three-million seller), a backlash was inevitable. The opening shot was fired July 12 at Chicago's Comiskey Park where, between the first and second games of a Chicago White Sox-Detroit Tigers double-header, radio disc jockey Steve Dahl blew up a mountain of disco records as part of a "Disco Demolition Night" promotion. The ensuing riot caused the second game to be canceled, and the "**disco sucks**" movement was off and running.

TOP SINGLES

The Knack
"My Sharona"

Donna Summer
"Bad Girls"

Rod Stewart
"Do Ya Think I'm Sexy"

Peaches And Herb
"Reunited"

Gloria Gaynor
"I Will Survive"

...And New Wave Breaks

Ironically, one of the year's biggest disco singles was released by veterans of New York City's punk scene. After their first two albums went nowhere, **Blondie** broke through to the mainstream with the blatantly discofied "Heart of Glass;" yet the band—along with such disparate acts as The Knack, The B-52s, and Cheap Trick—was widely considered to be "New Wave," the industry's shorthand term for more accessible (and apolitical) variations on punk rock. Though New Wave was hotly tipped to be "the next big thing," it turned out to have a relatively short shelf life. (The oft-repeated story that the Carter administration pressured American record companies to steer clear of the punk movement is probably apocryphal; more likely, the industry merely understood that most American rock fans were even more leery of punk than they were of disco.)

In other music news, **Bob Dylan** freaked out his longtime followers by converting to Christianity and releasing the dour *Slow Train Coming;* The Charlie Daniels Band unwittingly primed the world for the advent rap music with "The Devil Went Down to Georgia;" eleven Who fans died during a stampede for seats at a Who concert in Cincinnati, Ohio; and moustachioed singer-songwriter Rupert Holmes scored the last Number One of the "Me Decade" with the sleazy "Escape (The Pina Colada Song)." *Off The Wall*, **Michael Jackson**'s first solo album since the early seventies, was a huge hit, though it was in reality just a warm-up for his forthcoming blockbuster.

Movie News

It was almost too spooky to be a coincidence. *The China Syndrome*, a drama about an accident at a California nuclear facility (and its subsequent cover-up), had barely opened when the **Three Mile Island** leak occurred; the accident silenced the energy companies who had derided *The China Syndrome*'s premise as far-fetched, and lent an extra measure of terror to the Jane Fonda-Michael Douglas vehicle.

Even more frightening was ***Apocalypse Now***, Francis Ford

IN THE NEWS

January – The Shah of Iran is deposed by a fundamentalist dictatorship led by the Ayatollah Ruholla Khomeini. Suffering from lymphoma, the ailing Shah flees to Mexico, then to the US in October. When uproar over his presence there becomes too great, the Shah relocates to Panama.

February 8 – In an attempt to force Anastasio Somoza to negotiate with the insurgent Sandanista movement, President Carter severs military ties with Nicaragua, and threatens the reduction of economic aid.

March 28 – A near-disaster occurs at he Three Mile Island nuclear facility near Harrisburg, PA, when a power plant malfunctions, leaking radioactive steam into the atmosphere.

May 25 – An American Airlines DC-10 crashes in Chicago shortly after takeoff; 275 people are killed in the worst air disaster in US history.

June 13 – The Sioux Indian nation is awarded $17.5 million for lands taken from them in the Black Hills of South Dakota back in 1877; including interest, the settlement comes to over $100 million.

June 18 – The SALT 2 strategic arms limitation treaty is signed in Vienna by President Carter and USSR President Leonid Brezhnev.

July 15 – In a televised speech, President Carter calls for a new energy conservation program that includes limiting oil imports, reducing oil use by utilities, and the study of other forms of fuel.

'79 ***Above:*** **Debbie Harry, lead singer of Blondie.**

IN THE NEWS

September 23 – 200,000 demonstrators attend the "No Nukes" anti-nuclear rally and concert in New York City.

October 8–12 – The Dow Jones Industrial plunges 58 points in panic trading triggered by the Federal Reserve Board's raising of interest rates. Though the market eventually rights itself, the new high interest rates spell bad news for the automobile and construction industries.

November 4 – The US embassy in Teheran, Iran is seized by Iranian student revolutionaries. All foreign, black and female hostages are quickly released, but 52 white American males remain in custody. The revolutionaries demand the return of the deposed Shah to Iran in order to stand trial; the US refuses, and the "hostage crisis" begins.

December 4 – President Carter announces candidacy for re-election, despite polls showing his approval rating at its lowest levels yet.

TOP ALBUMS

The Eagles
The Long Run

Led Zeppelin
In Through The Out Door

Supertramp
Breakfast In America

The Bee Gees
Spirits Having Flown

Donna Summer
Bad Girls

Coppola's hallucinatory adaptation of Joseph Conrad's *Heart of Darkness*, which starred Marlon Brando as an out-of-control US officer in Vietnam, and Martin Sheen as the special agent assigned to kill him. And for sheer visceral thrills, you couldn't beat the worm-like creature busting out of a man's stomach in *Alien*, the sci-fi thriller that made Sigourney Weaver a star. Dustin Hoffman and Meryl Streep fought a custody battle in ***Kramer versus Kramer***, Woody Allen tried to make some sense of his romantic life in *Manhattan*, and Sylvester Stallone climbed back into the ring in *Rocky II*. There were some agreeable low-budget releases—Walter Hill's *The Warriors* was an evocative fantasy about New York street gangs, while Jonathan Kaplan's *Over the Edge* was a powerful look at disaffected youths in a suburban tract community. Not as good as it could have been, but still pretty damn enjoyable, was ***Rock 'n' Roll High School***, in which The Ramones played loud enough to cause deafness in white mice, and helped destroy a suburban high school in the process.

One of the surprise hits of the year, Blake Edwards' ***"10,"*** made a star out of Bo Derek, who played the object of Dudley Moore's affections. The statuesque Derek, the last of a string of look-alike wives for actor/photographer John Derek, inspired a mercifully brief infatuation among white women for corn-rowed braids.

John Wayne died of cancer on June 11, at the age of seventy-two, but at least "The Duke" could be content in the knowledge that America was still the land of the free and the home of competing roller disco films—both *Roller Boogie* (starring Linda Blair) and *Skatetown, USA* (with Scott Baio and Flip Wilson) tried to capitalize on the new fad, but with little success.

Palimony Acrimony

The other big news in Hollywood was the "palimony" suit brought against Lee Marvin by former girlfriend Michelle Triola Marvin. Though the couple had broken up in 1970, Ms Marvin claimed half the money Mr Marvin had earned during their six-year relationship. A judge eventually ruled against her, but did award her $104,000 for "purposes of rehabilitation."

TV News

To gauge the utter dearth of ideas in television land, one had only to look at the many new shows taking their cues from successful movies. ***Makin' It*** starred David Naughton (formerly of the "I'm a Pepper" Dr Pepper commercials) as the Travolta-like star dancer of a New Jersey disco, and was one of the few shows to in history be canceled while its theme song (sung by Naughton) was still in the Top Ten. (Naughton should have tried his luck on *Dance Fever*, a disco game show which gave out cash prizes to the best dancers.) ***Delta House***, a sanitized version of *National Lampoon's Animal House*, featured a handful of that movie's supporting players, but failed to hang on for more than a few months. Although John Belushi was still committed to *Saturday Night Live*, someone at CBS had the bright idea of cashing in on Belushi's new-found fame by casting his less talented brother Jim in the short-lived sitcom *Working Stiffs*, which also starred a young Michael Keaton.

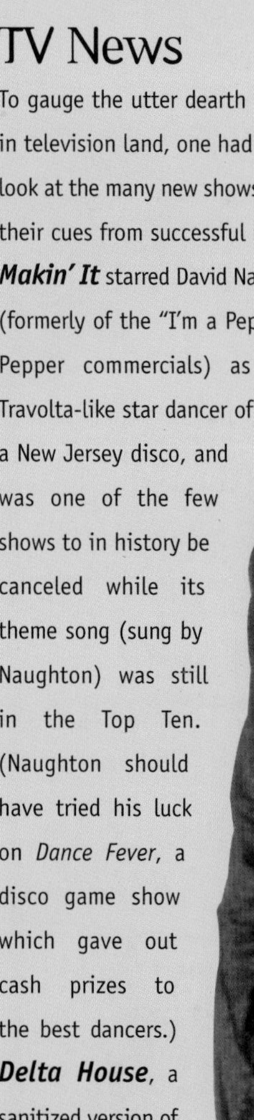

'79 Bo Derek.